CAPACITY

Receiving, absorbing, containing and reflecting more of Christ in a season of harvest

I0192097

12

"O God of wonder, enlarge my capacity to be amazed at what is amazing, and end my attraction to the insignificant."

John Piper

With deep gratitude to:

My soul-mate Helen and my two daughters, Elisha and Helga, who always assisted, encouraged and participated in the ministry God has laid before us;
A special word of thanks to Maureen Marud for her invaluable contribution in proof-reading the manuscript;
The amazing team at INcontext International for their support, friendship, sacrifice, assistance and encouragement;
Magdy and Annelise Saber, two people who have richly and abundantly contributed to capacity growth in my life and the life of my family.

Published by INcontext International
Email: mike@incontextministries.org
1st Edition: 2018

ISBN Number: 978-0-620-79068-0

"COME AND SEE"
A pre-reading precaution

I have discovered, regrettably through my own erroneous obstinacy and self-justified prejudice as a young believer, that the one single biggest obstacle to building capacity is selective learning; a false teachability that only accepts the teachings of those we agree with — or should I say those who agree with us.

We love to learn on a horizontal level where our uncertainties are never exposed, our fallacies never challenged, and our opinions always confirmed, even when proven wrong. We seldom venture into a vertical level of excavation where we learn from those who think differently than we do.

Think about the Protestant mindset rejecting Catholic teaching simply because it is Catholic, and vice versa. Or the reformed reasoning rejecting the charismatic experience, and vice versa. There are the conservatives and the liberals, the creationists and the evolutionists, the Orthodox and the Evangelical, the revolutionary and the pacifist, the pre-millennium and post-millennium, the persecuted and the prosperous – all reluctant to acknowledge that the other group might possess any wisdom that could be useful for spiritual growth. The doctrinal walls that block exposed wisdom are endless.

Even Jesus suffered under prejudice when He started His ministry because of where He came from, and His teachings were challenged even before He opened His mouth. "Nazareth! Can anything good come from there?" Nathanael asked. (John 1:46)

"Come and see!" said Philip.

My invitation to you as reader matches that of Philip. "Come and see. Don't shun the Nazarene. Be open to be challenged while you firmly hold on to your own convictions." You do not have to agree with everything written in this book, but don't disregard the "Nazarene" because of cultural or doctrinal prejudice.

In this book you will find quotes from all kinds of people, for good reason. Some are seen to be wolves in sheep clothing, but they still have some valuable wisdom to contribute. Some are described as Christian pagans, some are said to be ecumenical Roman Catholics, some are labelled part of the Emerging Church movement, some are described as being self-help gurus, some are considered New Agers and some even secular psychiatrists.

My invitation is as follows: After nearly 40 years in ministry I have learnt that the Lord has not limited His wisdom to Christians only. I have come to understand that God can even reveal His purposes to His prophet through the mouth of a donkey[1]. The challenge in the Biblical story of Balaam is not to look at the donkey for wisdom but simply to see it as the vessel of a Godly oracle. Balaam missed the point completely, as we so often do as well. It might do us all well at times to listen to those we disagree with (the "donkeys", in our eyes) in order to understand that the wisdom of God stretches further than our own theologies.

So why the need to resort to these un- or non-Christian sources when we have the wealth of Scripture from which to learn? Would it not be better to simply feed the reader with words from Christ and the apostles, rather than with stories from people who might not even be Christian? My answer is three-fold:

Firstly, this is exactly the same question the disciples asked Jesus (Matthew 13:10)[2] . "Why do you speak in parables?" And to make matters worse for those who followed the Teacher from a cultural position, was the fact that the parables often included pagans, the unsaved and enemies of the Jews:

---

[1] Numbers 22:28 Then the LORD opened the donkey's mouth, and it said to Balaam, "What have I done to you to make you beat me these three times?"
[2] Matthew 13:10-13 The disciples came to him and asked, "Why do you speak to the people in parables?" He replied, "Because the knowledge of the secrets of the kingdom of heaven has been given to you, but not to them. Whoever has will be given more, and they will have an abundance. Whoever does not have, even what they have will be taken from them. This is why I speak to them in parables: "Though seeing, they do not see; though hearing, they do not hear or understand."

Samaritans and Romans. Why not simply quote the prophets, why refer to those who were culturally and religiously offensive?

Jesus's primary goal was to educate and engage people in the Kingdom of God, not to teach Scripture *per se*. Jesus always honored and often idealized good, holy non-Jews, like the Samaritan man (Luke 10:29-37), the Roman centurion (Matthew 8:5-13), and the Syro-Phoenician woman (Mark 7:24-30). The intent of the religion He taught was never to bring about a greater schism between heaven and earth and divinity and humanity but to provide the links that joined the two together in the hearts and minds of people. The stories Jesus shared did just that. Jesus understood that sharing earthly stories with a heavenly meaning would be easier remembered and more clearly understood.   Stories always contain symbolism and analogies that people identify with (salt, bread, sheep, etc.) and their meaning was fairly clear in the context of His teaching. Jesus also recognised the fact that stories have a time-release effect; they plant seeds that sprout later. He frequently used this method to illustrate profound and divine truths so that the principles conveyed would be like seeds planted in fertile soil. The **Good Samaritan** is an excellent example (by the way, in the hearts of the audience this alone was a contradiction in terms. *Good* and *Samaritan* were not two words to be used in the same sentence). How many of us would have remembered the principle of loving our neighbour if it was not for the pagan Samaritan in the story of Jesus?

Matthew Henry explains as follows: *"A parable is a shell that contains good fruit for the diligent, but keeps it from the slothful. The disciples did not say, 'Why do you speak to US in parables? (they knew how to get the parables explained) but to 'THEM'. We ought to be concerned for the edification of others, as well as for our own, by the word preached; and if ourselves be strong, yet to bear the infirmities of the weak."*

Secondly, I am a firm believer that ALL wisdom comes from God even if it is uttered by those who do not fully acknowledge Him in a way that fits into our theological boxes. In Him alone **are hidden all the treasures of wisdom**

and knowledge[3]. I firmly believe we have much to learn from everyone on earth because every human being was created in the image of God with a certain sense of a God-understanding in their lives. BUT, in saying this, I do not imply that every word uttered by every creature on earth is truth. I therefore used the following criteria when quoting people in this book:

- Is the *principle* being conveyed consistent with Scripture? If it contradicts Scripture, then it is obviously not Truth and therefore not usable. All the "parables" (stories and quotes) used in the book are consistent with the Truth of Scripture. Nothing contradicts Scripture or the character of God. I am certainly not promoting the people I quote – I am promoting the principles of Scripture.
- Is the *attitude* endorsed consistent with the character of Christ? Does it promote the non-negotiables that Christ taught: forgiveness, peace, brokenness, simplicity, acceptance, etc?

Thirdly, I believe that God's truth is often revealed in cultures that do not know Him, and yet have a sense of God that we can learn from – not because of who they are but because of who God is! The "wolf-story" from a Cherokee Indian tribe on page 92 illustrates this principle.

So, "come and see!"

---

[3] Colossians 2:2-3 My goal is that they may be encouraged in heart and united in love, so that they may have the full riches of complete understanding, in order that they may know the mystery of God, namely, Christ, **in whom are hidden all the treasures of wisdom and knowledge.**

INDEX

INTRODUCTION

Luke 17:5 The apostles said to the Lord, "Increase our faith!"

CAPACITY, simply defined, is the ability to receive, absorb and contain.

One of the main challenges on the journey of faith is that we confuse the principle of transformation with the process of spiritual growth. We become, and then make, disciples who still operate, think like and conform to the patterns of this world (Romans 12:2) without being transformed by the renewal of their minds.

As Christians we need to be transformed with an ever-increasing capacity to develop a Christ consciousness. We need to be discontent to live a life of spiritual smallness, satisfied to fill our "small containers" week after week without any desire to increase our capacity.

We need to pursue lives of expanded capabilities to receive, absorb and contain as much of Christ as possible. And what we are able to absorb will eventually determine our output — that which we are able to give out or produce. The larger our capacity to be intimate with Christ, the more we will have the ability to reflect Christ and influence society.

This book was birthed in a market square in Tyre, 82 kilometres south of Beirut, Lebanon.

It was the Day of Ashura, one of the holiest days in Shia Islam, that commemorates the killing of Imam Hussein, a grandson of the prophet Muhammad in 680 AD, in Karbala, Iraq. Ashura is an annual event where Muslims march through the streets of Beirut's southern suburbs, some marking the day with a self-flagellation ritual called *TATBIR*, hitting themselves with chains and cutting their heads with swords and spears in mourning for the imam.

The market we visited was situated in an area where many Lebanese Muslims were preparing an arena nearby to celebrate the holy day. Hezbollah soldiers were well positioned throughout the market, clothed in their traditional uniforms, wearing the recognizable green headscarves, and unmistakably armed with AK47 assault rifles. Although shoppers were doing business as usual there was a sense that security was on high alert. As Westerners we sensed the tension all the more.

But it was not the presence of danger that gripped my heart, it was the absence of peace. My thoughts were still captured by the meetings we had the previous day with several Christian leaders from different regions in Syria. They were not refugees. For seven years they have faithfully ministered to the people of their regions through deep despair, severe suffering and extreme sacrifice. Though there were no words left to describe the destruction that millions endured, and are still living with, in cities like Aleppo, Homs, Damascus and Jaramana, the message we heard was not the one we expected. It was not a message of people lamenting their circumstances and bemoaning the fact that they were victims in an unjust society. It was not a group of people seeking solace in the midst of their hardship. There was a contagious excitement present in those we met. Without exception the one message they all shared was simply: *"THIS IS GOD'S TIME FOR SYRIA!"*

My faith was challenged. This was such a different message than the relentless reports from the news media that made us believe Syria was at a point of no return: More than **11 million** people uprooted and violently displaced: **50** families every hour for more than 5 consecutive years. More than **450,000** Christians fled the country while more than **250,000** people were killed during the civil war. A nation where **one person died violently** every 10 minutes in 5 years of brutal warfare between rebels, extremists and government militia.

Like the apostles I cried out to God: *"Increase my capacity O Lord. Help me to look beyond the obvious and lead me into the significant. Enlarge my spiritual capacity and my ability to look through Your eyes. Instil in me an understanding that seeks the redemptive when I look at the destructive. Develop my capacity to respond O Lord."*

There was one golden thread in all the testimonies we heard from the Syrian pastors. The message conveyed was not one of hardship but one of harvest. The war has become a conduit for building capacity. Pastor Ramih, a minister from Homs, shared how the war had matured believers and resulted in unprecedented growth in the Church. Zuka and Pierre, an elderly couple who serve in Aleppo, challenged our perception when they proclaimed that *"Aleppo is God's paradise."* And she explained why: *"This is where God is bringing souls into the Kingdom like never before."*

My capacity was both challenged and enlarged at the same time. Not only did a new anguish flood my heart but I also experienced a "light-bulb" moment of recognising a sovereign God present in all the hardship. Capacity growth and capacity building, I realised, are inseparable from a faith that is stretched and challenged to the limit. I had a new awareness that the greatest threat to a pursuit of spiritual maturity is a safe religion, nestled in freedom, that limits capacity development.

Standing in the market, sensing the conflict in my own heart between freedom and war, apathy and advance, and comfort and conflict, I realised the greatest — or one of the greatest — needs of our time is an increase in spiritual capacity. NOT an increase in Biblical knowledge. NOT an increase in spiritual leadership. But a capacity that will result in depth and stamina, unparalleled love and unconditional forgiveness, painstaking endurance and painful sacrifice, servanthood, humility, virtue and godliness. Sadly, these virtues are often a lost dimension due to an over emphasis on knowledge that tends to puff up rather than build up[4].
And this is *THE* challenge!

A BIGGER-BOTTLE-BELIEFSYSTEM

There was one other picture that emerged while meeting with the Syrian leaders — the fact that the Church in the west is often more obsessed with content than capacity. Through years of freedom and affluence the Church

---

[4] 1 Corinthians 8:1 Now about food sacrificed to idols: We know that "We all possess knowledge." But knowledge puffs up while love builds up.

in the West has increased in knowledge but at the same time decreased in capacity.

When Christ (Matthew 22:29[5]) encouraged His disciples to live an "error free" Christian life, it was a dualistic call, pursuing equal proportions of both knowledge and capacity; never one at the cost of the other.

Christians are often like empty bottles when we attend services and seminars, hoping to be filled with information and to leave as "filled vessels" with more knowledge than before to address the needs in the world. These meetings are focused on content more than on capacity.

What should happen is that we leave a service not with "FILLED bottles" but with "**BIGGER** bottles" and a capacity that has been stretched and enlarged. We need to enter a meeting with a 1-litre container of available volume and leave the meeting with a 5-litre container, with a greater capability to contain more.

As Christians we need to increase our capacity to develop a Kingdom Culture. We need to be discontent to live a life of spiritual smallness, just to fill our small bottles every Sunday without any desire to increase our capacity to be relevant in the season we live in.

The season we live in demands capacity building and capacity development. The question every believer should ask himself or herself is whether we are satisfied with standard capacity or do we desire an overflow capacity? When we discuss the Biblical mandate of unconditional love, do we seek to simply contain a volume of love in a vessel that will satisfy worldly definitions of love, or do we seek an overflow capacity that will fulfil the Biblical mandate to reach beyond the familiar into the realm that touches even the lives of our enemies? Our understanding of the difference between these two measurements will help us find the capacity that fits a

---

[5] Matthew 22:29 Jesus replied, "You are in error because you do not know the Scriptures or the power of God.

life worthy of following a Saviour who challenged His followers into lives of capacity development.

CONTENT AND CAPACITY

Standing in the market square and facing a reality that moved me beyond my comfort zones brought a new awareness of the unhealthy balance in the west between CONTENT and CAPACITY. Not that the problem is knowledge as such, or the accumulation of it; the problem is that too often we are taught just enough, meeting after meeting, to keep on believing what we have been taught in the first place. This creates an unhealthy contentment of just filling the same bottle time after time and placing a higher value on "what to believe" than "how to expand"! But this will require an intentional choice because content is absorbed while capacity is pursued.

It is guesstimated that Christians in the USA spend around **8 BILLION dollars PER YEAR** on mission conferences to TALK about missions. That's more than HALF the total spent on DOING missions.

Christians who enjoy the luxury of freedom tend to focus more on developing solid theologies and a firm Biblical knowledge, even on topics that are far removed from their experience, ranging from persecution, refugees, suffering, human rights abuses, modern day slavery and any topic you can talk about. We obtain a full grasp of the theology of suffering, even becoming experts in the field of persecution, without ever increasing our capacity to understand these theologies from an intimate, sacrificial and personal experimental level. We attend seminars and conferences on persecution in luxury hotels, willing to fill our "bottles" with knowledge but not willing to expand our capacity by sacrificing safety and comfort. We enjoy and preserve our freedom while speaking on subjects that increase knowledge but not capacity. The shallowness and superficiality of such spiritual capacity is tragic as we cheapen the sacrificial by emphasising the easy, the quick and the glamorous avenue of filling up with content.

The season we live in DEMANDS that we redefine our understanding of Kingdom and Church. The season we live in will present opportunities beyond the current capacity of the western church. In Luke 10:2 after Jesus told His disciples that, *"The harvest is plentiful, but the workers are few. Ask the Lord of the harvest, therefore, to send out workers into his harvest field."* He immediately commissioned them to *"Go!"* and He sent them out like "lambs among wolves." Content of the harvest and capacity to endure need to go hand in hand.

'CONTRADISTINCTIVE' CAPACITIES

But there is another component to consider in building capacity: BALANCE. Too often capacity growth is one-dimensional which leads to unbalanced Christians who develop spiritual muscles in one virtue at the cost of another. In this regard it becomes imperative to intentionally develop capacity in CONTRADISTINCTIVE virtues.

Be sure to read this word correctly: *CONTRADISTINCTIVE*. Not *"CONTRADICTIVE"*. In essence, this refers to two elements (such as virtues) that might seem contradictive at first, but are actually two distinct and opposite qualities that complement one another in various ways. Take the qualities of self-confidence and humility as examples: At first, it seems as if these two qualities might contradict one another, but together they become a powerful virtue in the life of a disciple. Building the capacity of self-confidence is an important path to maturity, but without adding the "contradistinctive" capacity of humility, self-confidence will lead to arrogance. In the same way, humility without self-confidence will lead to a low (and potentially destructive) self-image.

Contradistinctive lessons will ensure well-balanced and mature believers.

Let me elaborate. There is one critical pitfall that hides in the well-meant intentions of many theologians. It is not the danger of teaching unbiblical values, but teaching unbalanced values. This is hidden in the trap of focusing on selective Scriptures, selective teachings and creating a platform for selective capacity growth.

In his book, "The Sin of Certainty", Peter Enns writes the following[6]:
"In ways we do not even perceive, we all create God in our own image. We may mean well and we may be motivated by our devotion toward God. But even when these ideas about God have proven very helpful to us, they become a hindrance to growth when the cement dries. No one just 'follows' the Bible. We interpret it as people with a past and a present, and in community with others, within certain traditions, none of which is absolute. Many factors influence how we 'follow' the Bible."

The challenge of a well-balanced life often requires a strength in two proportions, not only one. It needs a theology of contradistinction. A tennis player who can play a brilliant forehand but struggles with his backhand will never become a champion. A bird with one strong wing and one weak wing will fly in circles. Being in a state of equilibrium is an absolute necessity for a properly-balanced symphony orchestra. A well-rounded student is not someone who excels in one subject only and has no proper knowledge in general.

When building capacity we need to understand that faith always has more than one component, and each distinctive component needs to be explored and developed at the same time, with the same urgency, in relation to one another and not at the expense of one another.

Think about it: Scripture is full of contradistinctive teachings and counter-balances:

- It teaches **prosperity,** but also **charity**
- It teaches **abundance,** but also **equality**
- It teaches **grace,** but also **works**

---

[6] "The Sin of Certainty: Why God Desires Our Trust More Than Our 'Correct' Beliefs". Harper One, 2016

- It teaches **joy,** but also **anguish**
- It teaches **healing,** but also **brokenness**
- It teaches **peace,** but also **war**
- It teaches **reaping,** but also **sowing**
- It teaches **truth,** but also **love**
- It teaches **release,** but also **endurance**
- It teaches us to **believe,** but also to **test**
- It teaches **urgency,** but also to **be still**
- It teaches **unity,** but also **diversity**
- It teaches **humility,** but also **boldness**
- It teaches about **bearing fruit,** but also about **pruning branches**

There are always two sides of every virtue that need to be enlarged and both need to be explored in the same measure. No one teaching of Christ should be placed higher than any other. The secret of capacity building is an equal emphasis on *all* virtues necessary to ensure God-glorifying life disciplines.

LEARNING TO UNLEARN

There is one final point before we commence. My personal journey of building capacity, although still a work in process, came more by unlearning old things than by learning new things. Creating capacity is not only about obtaining new and bigger containers but also about emptying old containers that have accumulated spiritual clutter through many years of cultural theology. The biggest limitation on capacity growth is very often existing convictions based on untested "truths".

Richard Rohr said the following:
*"God is not found in the soul by **ADDING** anything, but by a process of **SUBTRACTION.** The spiritual life is more about **UNLEARNING** than it is about **LEARNING.** It is only when we get out of our own way that the Lord can take over and fill us with greater capacity. But it's a gruelling process to come to this level of surrender, and few of us go willingly.*

*"But God can change us and the world if we allow the God of peace to **touch us**, disarm us, **heal us**, and send us out as instruments of God's peace. When you can become **little enough, naked enough**, and **honest enough**, then you will ironically find that you are MORE THAN ENOUGH. At this place of poverty and freedom, you have **nothing to prove** and **nothing to protect.**"*

The challenge therefore, as we embark on this journey, is to open our hearts not only to learn but also to unlearn, not only to believe but also to test and not only to add but also to subtract.

We need to apply the words of Paul in 2 Corinthians 13:5 *to examine ourselves to see whether we are in the faith and to test ourselves.* We need to remind ourselves of his instructions to the Church in Thessalonians (5:21) *to test all teachings, all revelations and all prophesies and to hold on (only) to what is good.* Holding on to the good also means to let go of the bad. We do not have the luxury to hold on to comfortable theologies that will soothe our consciences.

Neale Donald Walsch said the following:

"Yearning for a new way will not produce it. Only ending the old way can do that. You cannot hold onto the old, all the while declaring that you want something new. The old will defy the new; The old will deny the new; The old will decry the new. There is only one way to bring in the new. You must make room for it."

In writing this book I was personally challenged to re-evaluate my convictions and to align my "truths" with the character of Christ. I had to unlearn interpretations that were based on prejudice and let go of theologies that were built on a world-view of "right and wrong" that so often blurred my view of the true nature of Scripture. I had to make room for the new.

So, be ready to unlearn and be prepared to embrace theological modification if you are discontent with spiritual smallness and desire to develop a greater capacity to grow. Capacity growth will not come without sacrifice and only those who are willing to be confronted by themselves by embarking on a journey of self-denial will set new boundaries of spiritual growth. The book will address a holistic approach and look at twelve progressive steps to building capacity, one per month, in the following order:

1. **SPIRITUAL CAPACITY** — we need to move from a transactional faith to a transformational faith and pursue spiritual capacity to obtain a Christ consciousness.
2. **PERCEPTUAL CAPACITY** — once we expand our spiritual capacity we will soon discover the need to change our glasses and the way we perceive things.
3. **SOCIAL CAPACITY** — once we expand our perceptual capacity we will soon discover the need to consolidate our friendships and relationships
4. **INTELLECTUAL CAPACITY** — once we expand our social capacity we will soon discover the need to swop our shoes and adopt a scout mentality.
5. **MENTAL CAPACITY** — once we expand our intellectual capacity we will soon discover the need to modify our thinking.
6. **EMOTIONAL CAPACITY** — once we expand our mental capacity we will soon discover the need to align our affection with the non-negotiables of Christ.
7. **INTENTIONAL CAPACITY** — once we expand our emotional capacity we will soon discover the need to intentionally choose the way of the Spirit.
8. **GEOGRAPHICAL CAPACITY** — once we expand our intentional capacity we will soon discover the need to shift our boundaries and spiral into the unknown.
9. **RISK CAPACITY** — once we expand our geographical capacity we will soon discover the need to confront our fears.
10. **CHARITABLE CAPACITY** — once we expand our risk capacity we will soon discover the need to customise our budget accordingly and change our way of giving.
11. **BEHAVIOURAL CAPACITY** — once we expand our charitable capacity we will soon discover the need to restructure our actions.
12. **STAMINA CAPACITY** — and once we expand our behavioural capacity we will soon discover the need to tighten our grip, increase our spiritual

stamina, create new habits, transform our life-styles, acquire godly virtues and ultimately grow into full maturity.

*My prayer as we journey together is that along this journey to God, the self that **BEGINS** will not be the self that **ARRIVES.***

CHAPTER 1
Spiritual Capacity
We need to transform our faith

If your Christian conversion did not reverse the direction of your life, if it did not transform it then you are not converted at all. You are simply a victim of the "accept Jesus" heresy!
A.W.Tozer

Let's start by changing the starting point. We start with this simple yet profound truth: Change the starting point, and you change the trajectory; change the trajectory and you shift the destination. This is not only true in discrete mathematics but especially true for those who seek outcomes that will reflect a Christ resemblance through a transformational faith.

Building capacity starts with changing the starting point of our motives, our meanings and our methods. And even though capacity should be developed in all areas of our lives and no area takes preference over another, starting with our spiritual capacity will set a firm foundation for capacity growth in other areas. Once we are transformed by the renewal of our minds, it eases the process of developing a "building mindset" opposed to a "maintenance mindset". There must therefore be an expansion of our SPIRITUAL CAPACITY if we want to grow and mature as believers. *This will not happen by chance. It will happen by change.*

BUT NOTE: This chapter, and this book for that matter, is not about spiritual *GROWTH* – it is about spiritual *TRANSFORMATION*. Building capacity does not happen through more knowledge or even deeper insights into spiritual matters. Capacity growth happens when we confront ourselves, our life-styles, our values and our mindsets. Once we understand the difference between growth and transformation a new world opens up that leads us to embrace Christ in His fulness, not only His teachings.

Bill Plotkin offers a helpful model called the "Soulcentric Developmental Wheel." He describes eight stages of the spiritual journey of transformation. Plotkin says that most of mainstream Western society is at the third stage of adolescence, which is highly egocentric and narcissistic. As a culture, we tend to be preoccupied with our own comfort, entertainment, and security.

This is what we might expect of adolescents, but when people who are supposed to be spiritually mature still spend most of their lives focused on themselves, Christianity is surely in trouble. This is clearly seen, sad to say, in some Christian leaders who reflect our narcissistic culture rather than lead it forward. Robert Bly rightly called it a "sibling society."

Transforming from "sibling" to "adult" therefore becomes a matter of life and death for every follower of Christ. Sadly, it is possible to grow and not be transformed. I have met countless mature believers who know Scripture, love the Lord, seek the truth and have served faithfully in ministry but who are still "conformed to the pattern of this world" in the way that they think about other cultures, other religions, other races and "other" people who are different in their approach to life. I have seen how leaders and pastors with sound theologies respond to challenges in their communities and I have witnessed how few have really been transformed from puberty to maturity by the non-negotiables of Christ: love for adversaries, forgiveness for enemies, inclusivity for those who are different, etc.

An understanding of how the Western Church lost the emphasis on transformation and started focusing more on growth is offered by Richard Rohr as follows:

"Spirituality is primarily about human transformation in this life, not just salvation in a future realm. While Western Christianity lost much of this emphasis, and became rather practical and often superficial, the Eastern church taught theosis or divinization as the very real process of growing in union and likeness with God in this world. This is one of the many losses Christianity experienced in the Great Schism of 1054, when the popes of East and West mutually excommunicated one another. The later Protestant

Reformation, while needed, did not reclaim this wisdom and further split the church, each side losing something of value."

So, the early teachings of theosis and divinization changed into "making disciples", omitting the much-needed aspect of "Christ consciousness" and transformational components.

This is reflected in Church programs across the globe. If you Google-search *"discipleship training programs in churches"* you will find more than 4,3 million results. Not all are legitimate, I know, and some are duplicates, I understand, but nevertheless are endless in availability. And yet, I have still to visit one Church where there is an active, practical transformational program running. Not a training program with theories of how to be transformed, but practices of loving the loveless, practices of serving the destitute, practices of praying for the enemy. Not teachings in classes, but daily practices in the community of being transformed into the likeness of Christ. I have no doubt that they are there, but they are few and far between.

Be prepared therefore to be transformed, more than being informed.
It will be a sad indictment of any believer if we enter heaven the same way that we entered faith, only perhaps with a wider Biblical knowledge. Our theologies should be ever evolving, always increasing and continuously expanding in knowledge and in experience. Not because God changes but because our understanding and our position should be ever on a journey of new understandings and fresh revelations.

1 Corinthians 13:11 explains the process of an evolutionary theology and a continued modification of our theological position as follows: *When I was a child, I talked like a child, I thought like a child, I reasoned like a child. When I became a man, I put the ways of childhood behind me.*

As we start developing our spiritual capacity, the first step is to be transformed from an infant TRANSACTIONAL faith to a mature TRANSFORMATIONAL faith. Capacity development depends on this principle.

TRANSACTIONAL FAITH

For most of us the introduction to Christ was a "transactional" one. The Scripture in 1 Timothy 2:3-6[7] was received with great joy as we were reminded that *"God wants all people to be saved and that this happens through one mediator, the man Christ Jesus, who gave Himself as a ransom for all people"*.

We entered faith with a deep love for a Saviour who "gave Himself" and "paid the price" of our sins to become the sacrificial Lamb on our behalf. But if we remain transactional Christians for the rest of our lives we will never become transformed, changed and mature disciples. The process of transformation involves moving from loving Christ because He performed a transaction on the cross to being transformed into the likeness of the One who performed the transaction.

This becomes a major issue in expanding our spiritual capacity. The prosperity theology is a case in point. There is nothing unbiblical in the theology that God desires life and life abundantly for His Church. But this remains a transactional theology for spiritual new-born babies. What God desires of His Church is for us to be transformed.

Expanding our capacity to transform individually must translate into our communities as well. When we face droughts, crime, corruption, discrimination and injustice in our communities we hold prayer-meetings to appeal to our transactional God to intervene and restore. But we often neglect the transformational power of God that asks that we love our enemies, forgive our transgressors and reconcile with those who oppose us. Confessing Christ will seldom transform societies; living Christ will achieve far more than mere words could ever do.

---

[7] 1 Timothy 2:4-6 who wants all people to be saved and to come to a knowledge of the truth. For there is one God and one mediator between God and mankind, the man Christ Jesus, who gave himself as a ransom for all people. This has now been witnessed to at the proper time.

Too many Christians understand the act of salvation in a transactional way instead of a transformational way. This perspective allows us to ignore Jesus's lifestyle and preaching, because all we really need Jesus for is the last three days or three hours of His life. What we *GET* is for many far more important than what we *BECOME*. We convert the MASTER into a MASCOT, or some kind of genie that is ready at all times to respond to our needs and our desires. To enlarge our spiritual capacity will require an understanding of the life of Christ and not just an appreciation of the death of Christ. We need to move beyond salvation into transformation.

TRANSFORMATIONAL FAITH

Jesus is the most unlikely founder of a religion because he does not encourage any forms of sacrifice except the "offering" of our own egocentricity[8]. That message is hard to miss, but we turned the cross into a **TRANSACTION** and so missed its **TRANSFORMATIVE** message for humanity.

The definition of a transformational faith is probably best described by Cynthia Breault when she noted that: *"To be transformed is putting on the mind of Christ. It is not just admiring Jesus, but acquiring His consciousness."* When Christians are called to be transformed into the image of Christ in Romans 12:2[9] and 2 Corinthians 3:18[10], we are called to a process where we transform into the consciousness of Christ.

When followers of Christ are called to BE TRANSFORMED, Scripture uses exactly the same word as in Matthew 17:2[11] that describes the transfiguration of Christ. The Greek word used in all three these verses is

---

[8] Matthew 16:24 Then Jesus said to his disciples, "Whoever wants to be my disciple must deny themselves and take up their cross and follow me."

[9] Romans 12:2 Do not conform to the pattern of this world, but be transformed by the renewing of your mind. Then you will be able to test and approve what God's will is—his good, pleasing and perfect will.

[10] 2 Corinthians 3:18 And we all, who with unveiled faces contemplate the Lord's glory, are being transformed into his image with ever-increasing glory, which comes from the Lord, who is the Spirit.

[11] Matthew 17:2 There he was transfigured before them. His face shone like the sun, and his clothes became as white as the light.

met-am-or-fo-o which indicates a metamorphosis or a complete transformation in form and in nature – to be made new on the inside and on the outside. This is what we are taught in Ephesians 4:22-24[12] where the Church is instructed to *"put off your old self, which is being corrupted by its deceitful desires; and* **to be made new in the attitude of your minds**; *and to put on the new self, created to be like God in true righteousness and holiness".*

This is a transformational faith which does not refer only to "conversion" as a changing or entering of a belief-system but "conversion" as the process of changing or causing something to change from one form to another. Our spiritual capacity can only expand once we move from a "faith conversion" to a "life-style conversion".

One of the main challenges on the journey of faith, and often one of the most neglected teachings as well, is that we confuse spiritual growth with transformation. Most new believers are discipled in a process of reading Scripture more, listening to sermons more and getting exposed to Christian activities more. There is a process of growth that is mainly determined by information and not transformation. Converts feel more mature as believers as they grow in knowledge and even experience fruit on their respective activities. This is GROWTH, and even though it should be part of the process, it is not necessarily TRANSFORMATION.

Being discipled and being transformed are two completely different processes in the life of a believer and should not be confused with one another. You can be mature but still not transformed. However, you cannot be transformed without becoming mature. Capacity growth takes place once we transform and acquire the consciousness of Christ.

Transformation is to be a process of complete metamorphosis. We should talk differently, think differently, live differently, respond differently and

---

[12] Ephesians 4:22-24 You were taught, with regard to your former way of life, to put off your old self, which is being corrupted by its deceitful desires; to be made new in the attitude of your minds; and to put on the new self, created to be like God in true righteousness and holiness.

even look different. Scripture uses many different images to express the change that should occur:

- *2 Corinthians 5:17 Therefore, if anyone is in Christ, the **new creation** has come: The old has gone, the new is here!*
- *1 Corinthians 15:49 And just as we have borne the image of the earthly man, so shall we bear the image of the **heavenly man**.*
- *Ephesians 4:23 to be **made new** in the attitude of your minds;*
- *Colossians 3:9-10 Do not lie to each other, since you have taken off your old self with its practices and have put on the **new self**, which is being renewed in knowledge in the image of its Creator.*
- *Galatians 2:20 I have been **crucified with Christ** and I no longer live, but Christ lives in me.*
- *John 3:3 Jesus replied, "Very truly I tell you, no one can see the kingdom of God unless they are **born again**."*
- *1Peter 1:23 For you have been **born again**, not of perishable seed, but of imperishable, through the living and enduring word of God.*
- *Romans 12:2 Do not conform to the pattern of this world, but be transformed by the **renewing of your mind**. Then you will be able to test and approve what God's will is—his good, pleasing and perfect will.*
- *2 Corinthians 3:18 And we all, who with unveiled faces contemplate the Lord's glory, are being transformed **into his image** with ever-increasing glory, which comes from the Lord, who is the Spirit.*

Each of these Scriptures, in a different way, emphasizes the importance and significance of the change that is expected in the life of a believer. Not only growth but transformation. Each is as dramatic as it is traumatic and indicates a progressive process that is life-sustaining at the least or, if abandoned at any point, life-threatening. We are talking about a transformation that should be visible to others, but its internal effect should be far greater than what others can perceive.

Richard Rohr describes it as follows:

"The price for real transformation is high. It means that we have to change our loyalties from power, success, money, ego, and control to the imitation of a Vulnerable God where servanthood, surrender, and simplicity reign. Of course, most people never imagine God as vulnerable, humble, or incarnate

in matter. We see God as Almighty, and that vision validates almightiness all the way down the chain."

The process of metamorphosis is probably best described and best exemplified when a caterpillar becomes a butterfly. It embodies the principle that if a caterpillar grows without being transformed it will die as a caterpillar. Growth is not the goal of the caterpillar, metamorphose is. After all, who wants to remain a caterpillar, even a bigger and fatter one for that matter, if the beauty and glory of wings await you? Becoming new is the aim, taking on a different form is the goal. It gives a visual example of what transformation is all about and the process, spiritually interpreted, provides a powerful analogy of how to build capacity in this regard. To expand our spiritual capacity, we need to start with the egg, being born again, and then move to instar, to moulting, to pupa and finally to a transformed butterfly.

(The following steps of metamorphosis of a butterfly are taken from Butterfly School[13]).

EGG

Every butterfly begins its life as an EGG. Female butterflies are very picky about where they lay their eggs! This is because caterpillars are very picky about what they will eat! Each species of butterfly will only eat a single plant (or group of closely related plants) as caterpillars. This plant that a caterpillar must have is called the HOST PLANT for that species of butterfly.

John 3:3 Jesus replied, "Very truly I tell you, no one can see the kingdom of God unless they are born again."

Transformation begins with an egg. Nobody is born mature and nobody is conceived fully-developed. The discipling process begins with an egg. We might be well schooled in life and mature in years when we come to know Christ, but we now need to be transformed into spiritual maturity.

---

[13] http://www.butterflyschool.org/new/meta.html

Ironically, being "born again" as a grown-up can sometimes be more detrimental to our spiritual growth than if we were a child. The more we know the more there is to be re-formed and trans-formed through the process of first **unlearning** what we believed to be true.

But equally important in the **PROCESS** of being "born again" is the **POSITION** of being "born again" — where the eggs are laid. The new believer should understand from the beginning that they should be picky about what they eat. Transformation and growth will not depend on how much is eaten but WHAT is eaten. The HOST PLANT, the fellowship of belonging, should provide the right nutrition for healthy growth. Growing up on a poisonous leaf could be as fatal to a caterpillar as having nothing to eat at all. Growing up in a Church with unbiblical teachings and unsound practices could prove as harmful as growing up without any spiritual input at all.

Moving on now becomes a decisive part of the process. Staying a spiritual egg and being satisfied with spiritual smallness now becomes a major obstacle to future development and complete transformation.

INSTAR

When a butterfly larva (also known as a caterpillar) first hatches from its egg, it is very small! This young caterpillar is referred to as a FIRST INSTAR caterpillar. A caterpillar has only one job: to eat! Many species of caterpillars begin their feast by eating their egg shell, which contains plenty of nutrients. Other species of caterpillars immediately begin eating the tender, small parts of leaves.

1Peter 1:23 For you have been born again, not of perishable seed, but of imperishable, through the living and enduring word of God.

A new-born believer has only one job: **TO EAT**! So often we teach young believers that their first duty is to share their testimonies, to teach and to reach others with their new-found faith and to be trained as leaders. **EAT FIRST**. Transformation starts by digging into the Word and getting to know the transformational nature and character of the God we serve. There

33

needs to be growth before transformation. This process cannot be reversed.

MOULTING

Caterpillars face a challenge as they grow! Unfortunately, their skin cannot grow with them! In order for a caterpillar to grow larger than the skin it had when it hatched, it must make a new, larger skin! The caterpillar does this by first growing a new skin underneath the outer skin. Then, when it is ready, it "sheds" the old skin, and the newer, larger skin underneath is exposed. This process is properly called MOLTING. After the caterpillar has molted for the first time, it is referred to as a SECOND INSTAR, and it has some room to grow.

Romans 12:2 ... be transformed by the renewing of your mind. Then you will be able to test and approve what God's will is—his good, pleasing and perfect will.

This is so significant and yet so neglected in our teachings. We only truly become a new creation, fully transformed, when the old skin is shed. PUT OFF the old skin, says Paul in Ephesians 4:22[14] and PUT ON the new self! But it is a process. We often want to grow as new believers, but we don't want to drop our "old self". We still tell the same jokes, use the same language, complain like everybody else and blame our short temper on the fact that "that is how I was made". Transformation CANNOT take place if we cling to our old "skins", old habits and old natures.

But equally important is the fact that we first need to develop a new skin before we can be wholly transformed. If there are no new values formed underneath our "old skins" we have no new virtues to develop. The danger then is that we build Biblical principles on old values and we become self-

---

[14] Ephesians 4:22-24 You were taught, with regard to your former way of life, to put off your old self, which is being corrupted by its deceitful desires; to be made new in the attitude of your minds; and to put on the new self, created to be like God in true righteousness and holiness.

righteous and proud. We suddenly become aware of sin and become judgmental instead of broken and deeply aware of grace. New attitudes, values and principles need to be developed before we can just shed our skin.

But there has to be a time where we shed the old skin, where our life-styles, our world-views and our cultural values are transformed into new life-styles, a Kingdom world-view, and Christ-like values. Now there is room to be transformed.

Once again, we now have to move on.

PUPA

The chrysalis (generically referred to as a pupa), is not a "resting" stage as many people think. Quite to the contrary, a lot is happening to the pupa! The body of the caterpillar is transforming into an adult butterfly! Wings are fully formed (the beginnings of the wings were actually forming underneath the caterpillar's skin before its last molt) in the chrysalis. Antennae are formed and the chewing mouthparts of the caterpillar are transformed into the sucking mouthparts of the butterfly.

James 1:4 Let perseverance finish its work so that you may be mature and complete, not lacking anything.

To be transformed from MOULTING to BUTTERFLY will require a lot of work, unremitting action, sustained growth and painful endurance. This is not a time of "resting in the Lord" in preparation for "what lies ahead". We often want to protect new believers from the challenges and opposition that they may face when standing up for Kingdom values but we do more harm than good. This is a time of "building muscles" for "what lies ahead".

In a sense it is like the story of a man who found a cocoon of a butterfly and as he sat and watched the butterfly struggling to force its body through that little hole, he decided to intervene. He took a pair of scissors and snipped off the remaining bit of the cocoon. The butterfly then emerged easily. But it had a swollen body and small, shrivelled wings. The man continued to watch the butterfly because he expected that, at any moment, the wings would enlarge and expand to be able to support the body, which would contract in time. Neither happened! In fact, the butterfly spent the rest of its short life crawling around with a swollen body and shrivelled wings. It never was able to fly.

What the man, in his kindness and haste, did not understand was that the restricting cocoon and the struggle required for the butterfly to get through the tiny opening, were God's way of forcing fluid from the body of the butterfly into its wings so that it would be ready for flight once it achieved its freedom from the cocoon.

Sometimes struggles are exactly what young believers need. If God allowed us to go through our lives without any obstacles, it would cripple us. We would not be as strong as what we could have been. We would never fly.

Think about Saul on his way to Damascus when he encountered God and broke through his "earthly cocoon" into a transformed life with Christ. The first lesson he had to learn was to see *"how much he must suffer for My name"* (Acts 9:16). Do not disregard the "fluids" of suffering that prepare us for a greater capacity.

BUTTERFLY

After approximately 10 to 14 days as a chrysalis, the butterfly is ready to emerge. When the butterfly emerges from its chrysalis, its wings are small and wet, and the butterfly cannot yet fly. The butterfly must pump fluids from its abdomen through the veins in its wings, which causes the wings to expand to their full size. Next, the wings must dry and the butterfly must exercise flight muscles before it can fly.

2Corinthians 5:17 Therefore, if anyone is in Christ, the new creation has come: The old has gone, the new is here!

This is the pinnacle of our journey with Christ. Not being born again and remaining a "spiritual egg". Not growing in knowledge and becoming a "mature worm". But breaking free from the old and coming into the fullness of life as Christ intended, or, as Richard Rohr so eloquently describes it:

"The spiritual journey is a path of deeper realization and transformation; it is never a straight line, but a back and forth journey that ever deepens the conscious choice and assent to God's work in us. It is growing up, yes, but even more it is waking up."

BUT, let's pause for a moment: there is nothing romantic about the process. Comparing the transformation of a sinner turned born-again believer into a transformed Christ-like follower is both filled with beauty and romance. Or is it? The caterpillar's metamorphosis from a tree-clinging, 12-legged pest into the majestic flying butterfly is indeed a fantastic and awe-filled mechanism developed by nature, yet while all may seem fantastic on the outside, this transformation looks pretty gruesome, gooey and painful deep inside the chrysalis. In short, for a caterpillar to turn into a butterfly it digests itself using enzymes triggered by hormones, before sleeping cells similar to stem cells grow into the body parts of the future butterfly.

Metamorphosis isn't just some beautiful physical transformation. It's a stunning display of evolutionary mechanism at work. Butterflies and caterpillars don't just look different, they behave differently too. One lives in trees, the other flies. Most importantly, one eats leaves, and the other solely feeds on nectar.

This is the call of Scripture. Don't be content to be the crawling tree-clinging creature that so often presents itself as a follower of Christ. Pursue the process of digesting the self (die to yourself) and surrender to the stem cell as the Holy Spirit works new life, new attitudes, new love, new gentleness and new wings.

Many Christians are quick to mention the date or the occasion when they were "born again" and accepted Christ as their Lord and Saviour. But we shouldn't confuse the BUTTERFLY with the EGG. It is a different phase and a completely different process. Being "born again" is the time when we are conceived into the Kingdom of God; being transformed is the time when we are morphed into the consciousness of Christ. Being born again is the renewal of the heart while being transformed is a renewal of the mind. I have met few believers who could mention the date or event that started the process of transformation in their lives even though they knew exactly when they accepted Christ.

Being born again involves the heart and being transformed involves the mind. It is important to remember that we do not think differently because our lives are renewed; we live differently because our minds are renewed. The flow of behavioural changes starts with our thoughts. Thoughts lead to actions, actions lead to habits, habits lead to discipline, discipline builds character and character determines destiny.

Betsy McCrae from Glennon Heights Mennonite Church describes the act of transformation as follows:
"*Like a chemical imbalance in the brain, the value system of the world in which we live sends us powerful signals. These signals come fast and hard and have an immediate effect: 'You are what you own. You need more. Happiness can be purchased. Thrills are what you're after. People are not to be trusted. Life is dangerous. Violence is necessary. Protect yourself at all costs.' And on and on and on. One message after another. Endlessly racing, loud and bright. And sweeping us into a downward spiral of self-centeredness, loneliness, greed and despair from which we cannot escape.*

"*It takes a concerted effort to counteract these messages from our culture. It takes a concerted effort on our parts to change this pattern before it shapes who we are, before we are conformed to the value system of this world. It takes an effort much like the effort that folks living with depression or bipolar disorder have to make each day to keep themselves on an even keel.*

"If we truly want to follow Jesus, we must consciously choose to think differently. We must focus on Christ. All the time, in every situation, even when it is very difficult to do. And we must practice thinking differently until this new Christ-centred thinking becomes who we are, until instead of following the dictates of culture, we are offering our very selves and the lives that we live to God."

But, sadly, in the process of turning the egg (being born again) into a butterfly (being Christ-like) we often neglect the WAITING and the WORKING part of transformation. We want spiritually what we want materially; we want it all and we want it now. Too often in life I have seen young believers embarking on ministry only to be disappointed and disillusioned. They were never taught to **WAIT,** and they were never taught to **WORK.**

We need always to keep in mind two things about this transformation.

First, it is a process. It does not happen all at once. We "*are being transformed into his likeness with ever-increasing glory*". We spend a lifetime learning how to live by the Spirit, how to live a new life. We must "*work out*", and keep on working out, our salvation with fear and trembling. We must "*make every effort...to be holy*" (Hebrews 12:14)[15]. We must submit, and keep on submitting, to God. Over and over and over we must "*take captive every thought to make it obedient to Christ*" (2 Corinthians 10:5)[16]. Even near the end of his life Paul did not consider that he had arrived (Philippians 3:12)[17] and understood that he was still in the process of complete transformation.

---

[15] Hebrews 12:14 Make every effort to live in peace with everyone and to be holy; without holiness no one will see the Lord.

[16] 2 Corinthians 10:5-6 We demolish arguments and every pretension that sets itself up against the knowledge of God, and we take captive every thought to make it obedient to Christ. And we will be ready to punish every act of disobedience, once your obedience is complete.

[17] Philippians 3:12 Not that I have already obtained all this, or have already arrived at my goal, but I press on to take hold of that for which Christ Jesus took hold of me.

Second, we and God cooperate to bring it about. We cannot do it ourselves. And God will usually not do it without our cooperation. In this, as in so many aspects of our spiritual life, we and God are co-labourers. *"We are God's fellow workers"* as 2 Corinthians 3:18 clearly describes the relationship. *"And we all, who with unveiled faces contemplate the Lord's glory, are being transformed into his image with ever-increasing glory, which comes from the Lord, who is the Spirit."* And 1 Corinthians 3:9[18], *"Continue to work out your salvation with fear and trembling, for it is God who works in you to will and to act according to his good purpose."* We work and God works. We labour together.

One aspect of the transformation we seek is called showing the fruit of the Spirit. A farmer cannot cause the fruit to grow; he can create conditions favourable to its growth and protect it from parasites, diseases and other forces that seek to destroy it. In somewhat the same way, we cannot cause God's character to grow within us; only God can do that. But we can create favourable conditions for its growth — by faith, prayer, study of the word, etc. - and we can protect that growth from enemy attacks.

Transformation, to summarise, is not for the fainthearted nor the fearful. It is a process to life that will require death, but, as my good pastor friend, Richard Baird, once wrote: *"I think many Christians fail to understand a simple truth: the greatest sign and wonder that one could ever experience is the transformation of one's own heart."*

Amazingly, once we start building our spiritual capacity we will soon discover the need to build our perceptual capacity as well.

---

[18] 1 Corinthians 3:9 For we are co-workers in God's service; you are God's field, God's building.

CHAPTER 2
Perceptual Capacity
We need to change our glasses

Once we have started the process of being spiritually transformed we need to change the way we visually perceive and interpret our surroundings and our circumstances. There must be an expansion of our **PERCEPTUAL CAPACITY** if we want to grow and mature as believers.

Richard Rohr asks this question: *"Can you see the image of Christ in the least of your brothers and sisters? This is Jesus' only description of the final judgment (Matthew 25). But some say, "They smell. They're a threat, They're a nuisance. They're on welfare. They are a drain on our tax money." Can we see Christ in all people, even the so-called "nobodies" who can't or won't play our game (of religion)? When we can see the image of God where we don't want to see the image of God, then we see with eyes not our own."*

CLAY AND WAX

Before we begin to understand the link between the spiritual and the perceptual, we need to understand the link between the head and the heart. This lays a foundation on which all our attitudes, actions and affinities will be built. Spiritually, this is a matter of life or death.

I am often amazed at how diverse Christians respond to similar issues. This has been particularly evident over the past few years whenever the subject of the refugee influx into Europe comes into a conversation. There are those who respond with anguish and sympathy that reflects a willingness to pray and a readiness to reach out.

But there is always the argument that the refugee influx will ultimately result in the Islamisation of Europe and anybody who promotes any form of support is betraying "Christian Europe" and demonstrating a complete ignorance of the Islamic agenda of global domination.

Christians who profess the same faith, read the same Scriptures and worship the same Saviour differ comprehensively in their emotional interpretation of global events. Dominant convictions are either an attitude of anger or one of anguish.

I was reminded of a visit to Egypt where I questioned one of my dear brothers in Christ about the passage in Exodus 7:3-4 where the Lord proclaims to Moses that He will *"harden the heart of Pharaoh and then lay His hand on Egypt with mighty acts of judgment"*.

"Why would the Lord harden someone's heart and then punish that person for his hardened heart?" I asked my friend. *"This does not sound like a just God to me. Maybe, as an Egyptian, you have a cultural explanation for this Scripture."*

My friend smiled. *"You want to understand everything academically, Mike. In Egypt, we understand the natural implications of how a substance is hardened or softened by the heat of the Egyptian desert sun.* ***It will be the same ray of sun that hardens clay and melts wax.*** *It is ultimately not the ray of sun that hardens the substance but the content of the substance. It was not the Lord that hardened the heart of Pharaoh, but the content of his heart that hardened when God spoke to him. Our response to events will reveal the content of our hearts, and when God speaks to us, it will either melt our hearts like wax or harden our hearts like clay."*

This truth was a liberating revelation. It explains why some people are deeply touched by an issue and others angered; why some are filled with anguish when confronted with injustice and others moved to fear and anger. **It all depends on the content of the heart.**

More than ever the world needs a generation that will have the perceptual ability to view people, events and circumstances with hearts of wax. More than ever the world needs to see a generation that reflects **a God with a heart of wax.**

In 2 Corinthians 1:3 God is described as *"the Father of compassion and the God of all comfort"*. One of the most profound events in the Bible is found in John 11:35, where we find the Saviour of the world weeping next to a grave.

Christians have a mandate to imitate their Master by clothing themselves with hearts of wax. Colossians 3:12 states, *"Therefore, as God's chosen people, holy and dearly loved, clothe yourselves with compassion, kindness, humility, gentleness and patience"*.

This will be key to building capacity: That our response to global threats reflects hearts of wax and that we imitate and emulate a God who is known by His love.

But it is equally true in any perceptual observation that we cannot see what we do not give attention to. Perceptual Capacity will not only grow by "looking at the right things" but also by looking through the "right lenses".

If we suffer from inattentional blindness and do not give attention to finding GOD in global events, daily news, seasonal disasters and times of suffering we will never be able to expand our perceptual capacity to see a sovereign God at work. But it will also require a non-dualistic approach:

INATTENTIONAL BLINDNESS

Inattentional blindness is an inability to perceive something that is within one's direct perceptual field because one is attending to something else. This is very much an act of spiritual blindness as well.
The reality in life is that we will never be able to see what we do not give attention to. When watching the news or reading the newspaper our eyes will most probably see what our hearts want to hear and unless we

discipline ourselves to look through God's lenses, we will never acquire the ability to grow in our perceptual capacity.

In Matthew 13:13-15 the Lord speaks about inattentional blindness found in followers who were unable to perceive the hand of God in what was happening around them. These are the words of Jesus: *"This is why I speak to them in parables: Though seeing, they do not see; though hearing, they do not hear or understand. In them is fulfilled the prophecy of Isaiah: 'You will be ever hearing but never understanding; you will be ever seeing but never perceiving. For this people's heart has become calloused (hardened); they hardly hear with their ears, and they have closed their eyes. Otherwise they might see with their eyes, hear with their ears, understand with their hearts and turn, and I would heal them'."*

In Mark 13 (verses 5, 9, 23 and 33[19]), the Lord urgently warns His disciples to BE ON GUARD. The Greek word used here is *blep'-o,* which literally means *"to look at, to perceive, to regard and to take heed"*. The warning is therefore to not only look but to perceive. Not only to grow in knowledge but to increase in a capacity of "perceptual understanding".

Four times in Mark 13 the Lord tells His disciples to LOOK, PERCEIVE and TAKE NOTE. The understanding is that they should be like the men of Issachar (1 Chronicles 12:32), *"men who understood the times and knew what Israel should do"*. They were ready for action and on their guard. In a similar way, on this journey of faith, we need to continually grow in our capacity to perceive God's purposes in daily events.

SPOT THE GORILLA

In an article in the Smithsonian Mag[20], researchers studied the whole concept of perceptual invisibility known as inattentional blindness. In their

---

[19] Mark 13:5 "Jesus said to them: 'Watch out that no one deceives you.'"
[20] https://www.smithsonianmag.com/science-nature/but-did-you-see-the-gorilla-the-problem-with-inattentional-blindness-17339778/

best-known demonstration, they showed people a video and asked them to count how many times three basketball players wearing white shirts passed a ball. After about 30 seconds, a woman in a gorilla suit sauntered onto the scene, faced the camera, thumped her chest and walked away. Half the viewers missed her. In fact, some people looked right at the gorilla and did not see it.

That video was an Internet sensation. So, in 2010, they decided to make a sequel. This time viewers were expecting the gorilla to make an appearance. And it did. But the viewers were so focused on watching for the gorilla that they overlooked other unexpected events, such as the curtain in the background changing colour.

How could they miss something right before their eyes? This form of invisibility depends not on the limits of the eye, but on the limits of the mind. We consciously see only a small subset of our visual world, and when our attention is focused on one thing, we fail to notice other, unexpected things around us—including those we might want to see.

Indeed, most of us are unaware of the limits of our attention—and therein lies a real spiritual danger. For instance, we watch the news with political, cultural or religious preferences and fail to see the opportunities presented to us. We are so concerned about the corruption in our governments that we fail to see how the Lord is using the failure of man to point people to Him. We are so horrified by the war in the Middle East that we fail to recognise how thousands of disillusioned people are turning to Christ.

Building a bigger perceptual capacity will require an intentional removal of cultural and political glasses and a refocusing on Kingdom principles. There needs to be an awareness of Kingdom principles like salvation, forgiveness, love and inclusivity when observing global trends and a disregard for self-preservation and personal and cultural preferences.

However, expanding our perceptual capacity will not only require a mental shift, but especially an attitude shift

NON-DUALISTIC VISION

This is a challenging concept but critical in building a bigger perceptual capacity. Many Christians spend most of their lives organizing their theologies around what they believe, personal morality, and neat demarcations of who is "in" and who is "out" of God's favour and Kingdom. Most of our theologies are often based on "us and them". This creates a kind of "tribal" approach to religion, which refers to in-group/out-group thinking.

In an interview[21] with Father Richard Rohr[22], Ryan Thomas Neace addressed the issue of "non-dualistic thinking" and a working definition of dualism. Father Rohr answered as follows:

"The natural way the mind already "knows" as a child is in opposition to something else. It's funny that we have to have this explained to us, but you wouldn't know what "cold" was unless there was such a thing as "hot." If everything in the world was the same temperature, we wouldn't have these words.

"Unfortunately, we create those contrary words as necessary for the world we live in - that is, all kinds of comparisons, and competitions, and antagonisms... It becomes our primary way of reading reality.

"So, since this is the way we naturally think, very soon we tend to think oppositionally. For some strange reason, the ego prefers to make one side better than the other, so we choose. And we decide males are better than females, America is better than Canada, Democrats are better than Republicans. And for most people, once this decision is made, it is amazing the amount of blindness they become capable of. They really don't see what's right in front of them - everything has to be understood in opposition

---

[21] https://www.huffingtonpost.com/ryan-thomas-neace-/father-richard-rohr-on-ra_b_6606206.html
[22] Father Richard Rohr is the founder of the Center for Action and Contemplation (CAC) in Albquerque, New Mexico, and the author of more than 25 books about Christian spirituality.

to something else. Once you see this, it's an amazing breakthrough, and that is the starting place for moving away from dualistic thinking.

"This is why Jesus made so much of mercy, and forgiveness, and grace, because these are the things that, if truly experienced, totally break dualism down. Because once you experience being loved when you are unworthy, being forgiven when you did something wrong, that moves you into non-dual thinking. You move from what I call meritocracy, quid pro quo thinking, to the huge ocean of grace, where you stop counting, you stop calculating. That for me is the task of much of the entire spiritual life of a saint - they fall deeper and deeper into that ocean of grace, and stop all the counting of "how much has been given to me," "how much I deserve." It's reached its real low-point in our own (societies today), which is almost entirely about counting and deserving and earning — we call it a sense of entitlement. When you're trapped inside of that mind, you're going to have the kind of angry (communities) we have today, where you're just looking for who to blame, who to hate, who to shoot. It's reaching that level."

ORDER-DISORDER-REORDER

Richard Rohr continues to unravel the process of non-dualistic thinking[23] by calling the pattern of spiritual transformation a process of *"order-disorder-reorder."* Paul calls it *"the foolishness of the cross"* (see 1 Corinthians 1:18-25[24]). *"There is no nonstop flight from order to reorder,"* says Rohr. *"We have to go through a period of disruption and disordering. What we first call*

---

[23] Adapted from Richard Rohr, *Falling Upward: A Spirituality for the Two Halves of Life*

[24] **1 Corinthian 1:18-25** For the message of the cross is foolishness to those who are perishing, but to us who are being saved it is the power of God. For it is written: "I will destroy the wisdom of the wise; the intelligence of the intelligent I will frustrate." Where is the wise person? Where is the teacher of the law? Where is the philosopher of this age? Has not God made foolish the wisdom of the world? For since in the wisdom of God the world through its wisdom did not know him, God was pleased through the foolishness of what was preached to save those who believe. Jews demand signs and Greeks look for wisdom, but we preach Christ crucified: a stumbling block to Jews and foolishness to Gentiles, but to those whom God has called, both Jews and Greeks, Christ the power of God and the wisdom of God. For the foolishness of God is wiser than human wisdom, and the weakness of God is stronger than human strength.

"order" is almost always too small and too self-serving. The nexus point, the crossover moment, is one that neither conservatives nor liberals like or even understand. It will always feel like folly."

It is helpful for us to know about the whole arc of life and where it is leading. Walter Brueggemann brilliantly connects the development of the Hebrew Scriptures with the development of human consciousness[25]. Brueggemann identifies different stages in the three major parts of the Hebrew Scriptures: the Torah, the Prophets, and the Wisdom literature. He writes as follows:

The Torah, or the first five books, correspond to the good and necessary "first half of life." This is the period in which the people of Israel were given their identity through law, tradition, structure, certitude, group ritual, clarity, and chosenness. It's helpful and easiest for children if they can begin in this way. Ideally, you first learn you are beloved by being mirrored in the loving gaze of your parents and those around you. You realize you are special and life is good—and thus you feel "safe." Loving people help you form a healthy ego structure and boundaries.

Sadly, the opposite is also true. For those who grow up in an unloving, unsafe and insecure community, an unhealthy, aggressive and often violent character is established. These people are then viewed by those within the "healthy ego structure" as different, dangerous and sometimes even demonic.

The Prophets in the Hebrew Scriptures then introduce the necessary suffering, "stumbling stones," and failures that initiate you into the second half of life. Prophetic thinking is the capacity for healthy self-criticism, the ability to recognize your own dark side, as the prophets did for Israel. Without facing their own failures, suffering, and shadow, most people never

---

[25] See Walter Brueggemann and Tod Linafelt, An Introduction to the Old Testament: The Canon and Christian Imagination, 2nd ed. (Westminster John Knox Press: 2012, ©2003).

move beyond narcissism and group thinking. Healthy self-criticism helps you realize you are not that good, and your group is not the only chosen people. It begins to break down either/or, dualistic thinking as you realize all things are both good and bad. This makes idolatry of anything and war against anybody much less likely.

The prophets do not have much good to say about Israel, and thus seem to have all been killed (Matthew 23:31-32). Thus the "charism" of prophecy in its deepest sense has never been much sought after by most Christian groups.

Failing to recognise the prophetic stage in our own lives will result in name-calling, slandering and character defamation of those who are different to us and whose behaviour makes no sense within our "Torah experience" of a loving and caring environment. Capacity is limited and different world-views are seen as wrong, unbiblical and therefore not tolerated or accommodated.

The leaven of self-criticism, added to the certainty of your own specialness, will allow you to move to the third section of the Hebrew Scriptures: the Wisdom Literature (many of the Psalms, Ecclesiastes, the Song of Songs, Wisdom, and the Book of Job). Here you discover the language of mystery and paradox. This is what the second half of life is supposed to feel like. You are strong enough now to hold together contradictions in yourself, others, and the universe. And you can do so with compassion, forgiveness, and patience. You realize that your chosenness is for the sake of letting others know they are chosen too!

Only at this point do we learn how to hold opposing convictions without denying who we are. Here we learn how to respond to those who differ from us without reacting to their actions, words or threats.

More and more I am convicted in my own heart that it has become far too easy for me to refer to those who think differently to me as "them", while I safely hide in my "us" box, firmly defined by my "first half of life" experiences and carefully placed within the Christian walls of my convictions.

The current refugee influx into Europe could be one of the single most divisive issues of our immediate time. With the reality of the Islamic agenda in many people's minds, and widely different cultural worldviews blurring subjective views, many prefer to focus on the threats more than the opportunities. This is clearly revealed by the way fears are expressed relating to the refugee crisis: *"**They** come with an agenda; **they** come to Islamize **our** continent; **they** come in numbers and soon **our** culture will disappear."*

The word most often used in these arguments is also the one principle that most opposes the Gospel of Grace – ***THEY***.

The post-modern world has become a global village divided by "us" and "them", whether it be *"them"* the refugees, *"them"* the Muslims, *"them"* who are culturally/religiously/racially different from us, or simply *"them"* – those who do not fit into our boxes, defined by our cultural worldviews. Sadly, Christianity has become for some a safe haven with securely defined categories to snugly place ourselves into the *"us"* box. *"Them"* the sinners, *"them"* the unsaved or simply *"them"* the non-Christians gives us a moral system to fall back on that which distinguishes "us" from "them".

This dualistic thinking becomes one of the greatest obstacles to building a perceptual capacity. During a recent visit to Romania, an elderly gentleman approached me after a sermon and for no apparent reason shared the following thought with me. *"In a court of law,"* he said, *"there are always four role-players. There is the accuser, the defendant, the judge and the witness. Our role as Christians is not to accuse – that role belongs to the Accuser, Satan. Nor is our role to defend – that role belongs to the One who intercedes before the Father on our behalf – the Holy Spirit. Nor are we there to judge — that role belongs exclusively to the Father. We are called only to be witnesses."*

This short "sermon" greatly ministered into my heart. The Church is not to be primarily a loudspeaker, a megaphone on street corners calling out peoples' sins and taking a position on the judgment seat. We are simply instructed to be WITNESSES[26] and with a mandate to love God and to love our neighbour, we as the body of Christ are not to have the amplifiers blaring out from our hearts. The modern-day challenge for the global Church is to deal with the mentality of *"us versus them"*: those on either side of the megaphone. We can never, never, allow the Church to become an instrument of dividing "us" from "them".

BELONGING BEFORE BELIEVING

One of the most precious lessons I learnt from the persecuted Church in the Middle East is the principle of *"belonging before believing"* – that, regardless of whether we are "Jew or Gentile", we are all created in the image of God and we all share in the promises of God.

Travelling through countless countries in the Middle East I have come to an understanding that as Christians we have two wonderful things in common with all Muslims. Firstly, that we have all sinned and fall short of the glory of God[27] and that we are all saved by the grace of God through Christ Jesus His Son. We are therefore as much part of "them" as they are part of "us". We all belong to the same club of wretched sinners. As Christians we have no exclusive religion – there is no *"us"* and *"them"*.

Secondly, I came to learn that even though we do not **serve** the same God, we all **seek** the same God. Every Muslim I have met was on a journey of seeking God. The more radical they were, the more intent they were on finding God – misguided, yes, less serious, no.

---

[26] Acts 1:8 "But you will receive power when the Holy Spirit comes on you; and you will be my witnesses in Jerusalem, and in all Judea and Samaria, and to the ends of the earth."
[27] Romans 3:23 for all have sinned and fall short of the glory of God,

This understanding and principle of *"belonging before believing"* made everybody welcome at every meeting and at every opportunity. In the West, we have changed this Biblical truth to "believing before belonging". If you believe like I believe, then you are welcome. If you are a Christian, you can enter my borders; if not, you belong to "them" and you first need to become one of "us".

May we adopt the heart of Christ who, while we were still sinners, invited us to become heirs in the Kingdom. And even though this principle is not advocating or in any way embracing all teachings under one banner, it does proclaim that we are all sinners and fall short of the glory of God.

We are part of "them", but now know Christ by the grace of God.

Amazingly, once we start building our perceptual capacity we will soon discover the need to build our social capacity.

CHAPTER 3
Social Capacity
We need to consolidate our relationships

Faith is all about our social capacity. In the words of Christ Himself, true religion lies in loving God and loving our neighbour[28]. Everything else — doing good, knowing good and speaking good hang on this principle. We can never be authentic followers of Christ outside a community of people. There must therefore be an expansion of our **SOCIAL CAPACITY** if we want to grow and mature as believers. This is non-negotiable.

As human beings we exist in an entirely relational universe where, as Richard Rohr explains, *"energy is not in the planets or in the protons or neutrons, but in the relationship between them. Not in the particles but in the space between them. Not in the cells of organisms but in the way the cells feed and give feedback to one another. If, at any time, we try to stop this life- flow moving through us, with us, and in us, we fall into the true state of sin"*

Rohr then calls believers to move from a society dominated by individuality, greed, and competition—often resulting in oppressive economic systems, unnecessary suffering, and environmental devastation, to a community dominated by a network of relationships.

When we place our focus more on relational networks than economical networths, we start building capacity.

---

[28] Matthew 22:37-40 Jesus replied: "'Love the Lord your God with all your heart and with all your soul and with all your mind.' This is the first and greatest commandment. And the second is like it: 'Love your neighbor as yourself.' All the Law and the Prophets hang on these two commandments."

However, with the exponential growth of social media the challenge in building a wider social capacity lies not in obtaining more friends, but in developing deeper relationships.

One of the greatest gifts any person can pray for is loyal and faithful friends. Nothing on earth is more precious, more worthwhile investing in and worthier of keeping. Expanding our social capacity will to a large extent depend on our ability to make true and reliable friends out of acquaintances. It is often said that one's network determines one's net worth. It is also true that the quality of friendship one has determines the quality of one's life (Proverbs 13:20)[29]. Jesus grew in favour with God and also with men. In order to have an enhanced social capacity, one must seek true friendship with God and also true friendship with man; one must be a giver and not just a taker; and one must be free of pretence and shallowness.

The challenge in an age of unlimited technology is that we often seek friends that very often limit our capacity instead of expanding it.

un-SOCIAL MEDIA

With the rise of modern computing, social networks and "friendship circles" can now be measured and converted into a visual form, giving researchers the ability to study them on a much wider, even global, scale.

Continuing this tradition of social network research, Facebook, in collaboration with researchers at the University degli Studi di Milano, recently released two studies of the Facebook social graph. They measured how many friends people have, and found that this distribution differs significantly from previous studies of large-scale social networks.

Research on conventional social networks proposes that the number of people with whom an individual maintains close relationships is about 10-

---

[29] Proverbs 13:20 Walk with the wise and become wise, for a companion of fools suffers harm.

20 people. However, in studies conducted by Facebook in 2011, where they examined all 721 million active Facebook users (more than 10% of the global population), with 69 billion friendships among them, they found that 50% (the average) have over 100 friends with an average Facebook user having 190 friends. Yet, there are users on Facebook that acquire hundreds of these social connections; some have been seen to mount up to 500, if not more. These possibly weak ties have been explained to serve the purpose of bridging social capital rather than creating close kinds of relationships.

The irony with Facebook is that even though it has expanded the ability to add friends it has limited the social capacity of building relationships.

The Editor of the New York Times Book Review Pamela Paul[30] describes how social media *"has upended social and psychological norms"* by changing the meaning of some words to their opposite, or at least giving them a very different gist than they initially had. With Facebook, "to friend" has become a verb, and yet to do so, in the social-media sense, is a fairly passive act. In real life, when a friendship ruptures, it's a major event. But just as it's easy to start a Facebook relationship, it's virtually effort-free to end one. The personal investment on either side of "unfriending" somebody is infinitely lower than offline. *"The whole concept of what it is to make a friend has shifted,"* she explained.

For the 71% of Internet users now on Facebook, the word "friend" includes much more tenuous associations—old classmates, colleagues, one-night stands, in some cases, people who might otherwise be complete strangers.

Facebook places every type of social connection into a single "friend" basket. But relationship categories can serve an important function: An acquaintance versus a true friend, for example, signals different levels of trust and expectations. As 70% of Facebook users are on the site daily, sociologists and psychologists are examining the link between Facebook use

---

[30] https://www.theatlantic.com/health/archive/2015/02/how-real-are-facebook-friendships/384780/

and changes in relationship strength. Facebook may simply prolong superficial connections that would have naturally dissipated otherwise. It therefore becomes a capacity blocker instead of a capacity builder.

It seems like friendship builders are often relationship destroyers and reverting back to the old model of friendships seems to be the only way to build a social capacity. This will require investing time, emotions, resources and effort into developing, maintaining and keeping relationships; all commodities that are quickly disappearing in an age of technology.
In this regard there are 4 *FOUR*s to consider:

- Firstly, let us consider how closely we are all linked together: **FOUR DEGREES OF SEPARATION**
- Secondly, let us consider how we can link more closely together: **FOUR DEVOTEES OF UNIFICATION**
- Thirdly, let us consider how we link together when we are close: **FOUR DIVISIONS OF ATTRACTION**
- Fourthly, let us consider how we can get closer when we are not linked together: **FOUR DIRECTIONS OF ASSOCIATION**

FOUR DEGREES OF SEPARATION[31]

First, let us consider how closely we are all linked together.

Think back to the last time you were in a crowded airport in another country or even in a local shopping centre. Have you ever considered that the stranger sitting next to you or standing next to you at the counter could be linked to you by a short chain of acquaintances? Through modern technology it is quite possible that the person next to you could be the Facebook friend of a Facebook friend that knows a Facebook friend of a Facebook friend of yours. This is simply called FOUR DEGREES of separation and part of the "small-world phenomenon" that was an experimental study by Stanley Milgram in the 1960s. The subsequent studies after the discovery of the World Wide Web have confirmed that we live in a global village

---

[31] https://www.facebook.com/notes/facebook-data-team/anatomy-of-facebook/10150388519243859

where we are all linked to one another through four "hops" of friendships at the most.

In the 1960s, social psychologist Stanley Milgram's "small world experiment" famously tested the idea that any two people in the world are separated by only a small number of intermediate connections, arguably the first experimental study to reveal the surprising structure of social networks.

This idea was originally known as the "six degrees of separation" — that any two people are on average separated by no more than six intermediate connections. Milgram selected 296 volunteers and asked them to dispatch a message to a specific individual, a stockholder living in the Boston suburb of Sharon, Massachusetts. The volunteers were told that they couldn't send the message directly to the target person (unless the sender knew them personally), but that they should route the message to a personal acquaintance that was more likely than the sender to know the target person. Milgram found that the average number of intermediate persons in these chains was 5.2 (representing about 6 hops). The experiment showed that not only are there few degrees of separation between any two people, but that individuals can successfully navigate these short paths, even though they have no way of seeing the entire network.

Today, the scale and international reach of Facebook allows us to finally perform this study on a global scale. Using state-of-the-art algorithms developed at the Laboratory for Web Algorithmics of the Università degli Studi di Milano, they were able to approximate the number of hops between all pairs of individuals on Facebook. They found that six degrees actually overstates the number of links between typical pairs of users: While 99.6% of all pairs of users are connected by paths with 5 degrees (6 hops), 92% are connected by only four degrees (5 hops). And as Facebook has grown over the years, representing an ever-larger fraction of the global population, it has become steadily more connected. The average distance in 2008 was 5.28 hops, while now it is 4.74.

Thus, when considering even the most distant Facebook user in the Siberian Desert or the Peruvian rainforest, a friend of your friend probably knows a friend of their friend. When we limit our analysis to a single country, be it the US, Sweden, Italy, or any other, we find that the world gets even smaller, and most pairs of people are only separated by 3 degrees (4 hops).

It is important to note that while Milgram was motivated by the same question (how many individuals separate any two people), these numbers are not directly comparable; his subjects only had limited knowledge of the social network, while we have a nearly complete representation of the entire thing. Our measurements essentially describe the shortest possible routes that his subjects could have found.

In layman's terms, FOUR DEGREES OF SEPARATION simply confirms the "small-world-phenomenon" that social networks and people connectedness have exponentially expanded over the past few years. This means it's easier to make new friends, to find new friends and to break old relationships. To expand and develop our social capacity now needs extra time and effort, two commodities that are scarce in our fast-paced society.

It also means that the "ends of the earth" Jesus referred to in Acts 1:8[32] when He instructed His disciples to influence the global scene as His witnesses, are now only 4 hops away. And this is where it becomes critically important to invest in our circles of friends if we want to expand our social capacity.

FOUR DEVOTEES OF UNIFICATION

Secondly, let us consider how we can link more closely together.

We often think that we need perfect friends to build perfect relationships and secure perfect growth. When looking at Christ and how He chose His

---

[32] Acts_1:8 But you will receive power when the Holy Spirit comes on you; and you will be my witnesses in Jerusalem, and in all Judea and Samaria, and to the ends of the earth."

friends and the people He surrounded Himself with the answer is clear that He was looking, not for royalty but loyalty, not for flawlessness but faithfulness.

What is most amazing about the disciples is that among all the "righteous and religious" people Jesus had access to, He chose a handful of common fishermen, a hated tax collector, and an impulsive political zealot. They were a group of ordinary guys and, as John MacArthur writes in his book "Twelve ordinary men"[33], remarkably unremarkable and 100% human. But in their relationship to one another they became devotees and part of a unified force that forever changed the world.

But John MacArthur explores the friendship levels of Jesus not by looking at His countless followers or even His circle of twelve close devotees, but the fact that Jesus also chose an inner circle of three close friends, James, Peter and John, with whom He shared His deepest times of joy and deepest times of despair.

These four "soul-mates" were capacity builders in one another's life and as much as the three disciples needed Jesus, Jesus needed them. It was these intimate sessions together where Jesus prepared His three devotees to build capacity for lives of selfless devotion. But it was also in these intimate times that the three provided the solace and affirmation to their Master and Friend that He needed most.

- It was Peter, James and John that experienced the **AWE OF GOD** as they witnessed a voice from heaven confirming that Christ was the Son of God with whom the Father was well pleased.[34]

---

[33] Twelve ordinary men by John Mc Arthur - Published November 18th 2002 by Thomas Nelson

[34] Matthew 17:1-6 Six days later Jesus took with him Peter and the brothers James and John and led them up a high mountain where they were alone. As they looked on, a change came over Jesus: his face was shining like the sun, and his clothes were dazzling white. Then the three disciples saw Moses and Elijah talking with Jesus. So Peter spoke up and said to Jesus, "Lord, how good it is that we are here! If you wish, I will make three tents here, one for you, one for Moses, and one for Elijah." While he was talking, a shining cloud came over them, and a voice from the cloud said, "This is my own dear

- It was Peter, James and John that experienced the **POWER OF GOD** when the daughter of Jairus was raised from the dead[35]
- It was Peter, James and John, this time with Andrew, that were instructed to an alertness to the **TIMEFRAME OF GOD** when they sat together and discussed the unravelling of future events.[36]
- And finally, it was Peter, James and John that identified with the **SUFFERING OF GOD** when they watched their Friend in agony in the garden of Gethsemane[37].

Four close friends who witnessed fear together, shared miracles together, planned the future together and watched in terror as one of their own prepared for His death.

Nothing can outlive, outlast or outsmart those who devote themselves to one another, and together to God. To build a deeper capacity in a social context will require an inner circle of trusted people who will share our victories, failures, fears and joys with one another, and feel safe in doing that.

Son, with whom I am pleased---listen to him!" When the disciples heard the voice, they were so terrified that they threw themselves face downward on the ground.

[35] Mark 5:37-42 Jesus allowed no one to go further with him except Peter, James, and John, the brother of James. When they came to the home of the synagogue leader, Jesus saw mass confusion. People were crying and sobbing loudly. He entered the house and said to them, "Why all this confusion and crying? The child isn't dead but is sleeping." They laughed and laughed at him. But he forced all of them outside. Then he took the child's father and mother, along with the men who were with him, and went into the room where the child was. He took her by the hand and said to her, "Talitha koum," which means, "Little girl, I tell you, get up!" The little girl got up at once and started to walk, for she was twelve years old. Instantly they were overcome with astonishment.

[36] Mark 13:3 Jesus was sitting on the Mount of Olives, across from the Temple, when Peter, James, John, and Andrew came to him in private. (12) Men will hand over their own brothers to be put to death, and fathers will do the same to their children. Children will turn against their parents and have them put to death. Everyone will hate you because of me. But whoever holds out to the end will be saved. (35) Watch, then, because you do not know when the master of the house is coming---it might be in the evening or at midnight or before dawn or at sunrise. If he comes suddenly, he must not find you asleep. What I say to you, then, I say to all: Watch!"

[37] Mark 14:33 He took Peter, James, and John with him. Distress and anguish came over him, and he said to them, "The sorrow in my heart is so great that it almost crushes me. Stay here and keep watch."

Before you continue, put down the book, phone a friend and tell him or her how special they are.

FOUR DIVISIONS OF ATTRACTION

Thirdly, let us consider how we link together when we are close.

Relationships can generally be grouped into four divisions:
1. those that subtract,
2. those that divide,
3. those that add and
4. those that multiply.

If we truly seek to develop our social capacity it is wise to attract friendships that add and multiply value to us, and to shun relationships that subtract and divide us. We should avoid those that drain life and seek those that give life.

But it is equally important to pursue relationships where we add and multiply value into the lives of friends without seeking only friendships in which we are the beneficiaries. Capacity building is always a mutual exercise, it should never be only one party that benefits. Faith always inspires faith, courage inspires courage and boldness inspires boldness. As much as we need friends who inspire us we need to be that friend who inspires others.

To enlarge a social capacity will require that we move back to the old model of friendships where we invest our lives in like-minded people who we trust to be friends such as described in Proverbs:

- **Proverbs 12:26 talks about Godly friends**
  The righteous choose their friends carefully, but the way of the wicked leads them astray.
- **Proverbs 17:17 talks about loyal friends**
  A *friend loves always, and a brother is born for a time of adversity.*
- **Proverbs 18:24 talks about faithful friends**

One who has unreliable friends soon comes to ruin, but there is a friend who sticks closer than a brother.

- **Proverbs 20:6 talks about reliable friends**
  Many claim to have unfailing love, but a faithful person who can find?
- **Proverbs 22:11talks about pure friends**
  One who loves a pure heart and who speaks with grace will have the king for a friend.
- **Proverbs 27:5-6 talks about sincere friends**
  Better is open rebuke than hidden love. Wounds from a friend can be trusted, but an enemy multiplies kisses.
- **Proverbs 27:9 talks about honest friends**
  Perfume and incense bring joy to the heart, and the pleasantness of a friend springs from their heartfelt advice.
- **Proverbs 27:17 talks about involved friends**
  As iron sharpens iron, so one friend sharpens another.

FOUR DIRECTIONS OF ASSOCIATION

Fourthly, let us consider how we can get closer when we are not linked together.

Apart from finding comfort and security among like-minded people, it is also necessary to move outside the comfort zones provided by our cultural, economic, religious and political borders. To expand our social capacity will need an intentional effort to make friends outside our natural circles, defined by culture and preference. We need the ability to continually make new friends, from different cultures and different orientations. Four guidelines for seeking new capacities are as follows:

- **Make friends outside your socioeconomic borders**
  It is an amazing **"gratitude-builder"** to be with people who make do with less than you have. Making friends with someone who has less than you, will not only enlarge your social capacity but will also enlarge

your understanding of what really matters in life. But the challenge is to be a friend and not a bank.

- **Make friends outside your religious borders**
It is an amazing "**faith-builder**" to befriend someone with other religious convictions. This does not only entail befriending someone from another denomination but especially someone from another faith. When you befriend someone from another faith, you become more aware of your own faith and the joy of having a Saviour. It's when you get comfortable sharing your beliefs and values with others that you are open to learn from others as well.

- **Make friends outside your political borders**
It is an amazing "**conviction-builder**" to befriend someone with other political convictions. It's a gift to be able to listen to other convictions, understand the reasoning and still hold on to your own. It is liberating to have friends who do not share your political convictions and to be able to discuss it with mutual respect.

- **Make friends outside your cultural borders**
It is an amazing "**bias-examiner**" to build friendships outside our cultural borders. Few people have the ability to go through life without a bias against another group, gender, race, class, or religion. The only way to overcome the unbiblical attitude of "cultural pride", being snobbish and proud, is by befriending someone from a culture that you can least identify with. Try it. A whole new world will open to you.

BE AWARE AND BEWARE

There is one final and yet critical point to consider if we aim to expand our social capacity: It is the destructive and toxic habits of slander and gossip.

Psalm 15 "LORD, who may dwell in Your sacred tent? Who may live on Your holy mountain? The one whose walk is blameless, who does what is righteous, who speaks the truth ..., whose tongue utters no slander, who does no wrong to a neighbour, and casts no slur on others."

The two obstacles that can so easily and so rapidly destroy all our efforts to build our social capacity are **slander and gossip**.   John J. Edwards III describes gossip as follows: *"it's the greasy fast food of conversation, cheap, easy and bursting with uncomplicated appeal."*   The mystic world of spiritual power accompanied with rumours and suspicion will always result in gossip and eventually slander, which is taken as a serious offence by God and is completely unbiblical.

Slander among believers was described by Frederick William Faber in his classic *Spiritual Conferences*, as follows: *"Devout people are, as a class, the least kind of all classes. Religious people are an unkindly lot. Men may be charitable, yet not kind; merciful, yet not kind; self-denying, yet not kind. If they would add a little common kindness to their uncommon graces, they would convert 10 where they now only abate the prejudices of one. There is a sort of spiritual selfishness in devotion, which is rather to be regretted than condemned.   Kindness, as a grace, is certainly not sufficiently cultivated, while the self-gravitating, self-contemplating, self-inspecting parts of the spiritual life are cultivated too exclusively."*

David Aikman, in an editorial in *Christianity Today*, discussed how no attribute of civilized life seems more under attack than civility. He noted the extent to which certain Christians have turned themselves into the... *"self-appointed attack dogs of Christendom. They seem determined to savage not only opponents of Christianity, but also fellow believers of whose doctrinal positions they disapprove. A troll through the Internet reveals websites so drenched in sarcasm and animosity that an agnostic, or a follower of another faith tradition interested in what it means to become a Christian, might be permanently disillusioned."*

Francis Schaeffer observed the following toward the end of his life: *"We rush in, being very, very pleased, it would seem at times, to find other men's mistakes. We build ourselves up by tearing other men down... we love the smell of blood, the smell of the arena, the smell of the bullfight... We may be pleased, but we are not being Christian."*

Before spreading unverified information, and even when sharing factual information, first identify the type of gossip it might be. Jenn Johns outlined different types of gossip as follows[38]:

- **IS IT SLANDER?** This is defined as spreading rumours or lies about a person to cause damage intentionally. The Bible mentions slander countless times and tells it straight in James 4:11: *"Brothers, do not slander one another."*

- **IS IT DISHING?** "Dishing the dirt" basically means sharing the "juicy info" you learnt about someone. Maybe the intent is to "warn someone" but by keeping the gossip alive, it continues to spread and taint the image of the person. This is dangerous and unbiblical. *Proverbs 20:19 tells us that a gossip betrays a confidence; so avoid a man who talks too much.*

- **IS IT A RUMOUR?** You hear something, and it's not good, and it's also not confirmed as true. But you tell someone or ask someone else about it to get more info. The rumour mill turns and turns and the gossip spreads. Proverbs 13:3 says, *"He who guards his lips guards his life, but he who speaks rashly will come to ruin."*

- **IS IT BACKBITING?** It's a flavour of gossip that involves speaking spiteful or slanderous words about another who is not present and can do nothing in defence. It's secretive, and the Bible has a warning in this regard: *Psalm 101:5 says "Whoever secretly slanders his neighbour, him I will destroy..."*

- **IS IT PLANTING SEEDS?** The Bible tells us we reap what we sow. With that in mind, this type of gossip is said in such a way to make the

---

[38] http://goingbyfaith.com/types-of-gossip/

listener question or assume something about the character of a person. A warning from the Bible from Proverbs 16:28: *"A perverse man stirs up dissension, and a gossip separates close friends."*

- **IS IT WHISPERED INNUENDO?** These subtle insinuations can mislead others into thinking wrong thoughts, especially if the conclusions are based on gossip. Another warning from the Bible: *"What you have said in the dark will be heard in the daylight, and what you have whispered in the ear in the inner rooms will be proclaimed from the roofs"* (Luke 12:3).

- **IS IT I-GOT-THIS-ALL-WRONG GOSSIP?** You admit you probably got it wrong, but spread it anyway, because it's touching on some points that could be true. This is one of the most common types of gossip. We think we're just passing on the latest news. Does it matter? James 4:17 says, *"Anyone, then, who know the good he ought to do and doesn't do it, sins."*

What then should we share? Ask yourself the three questions as explained by Elizabeth Foss.[39]

- **IS IT TRUE?** This means we **STOP** before passing along hearsay or gossip. It also means that we hold a grand story up to the exaggeration test. This is also the filter that says we won't listen to gossip, nor will we pass it along. (*Exodus 23:1 "Do not spread false reports..."*) Once we have established the truth we move on to filter number two.

- **IS IT KIND?** It is too easy to use TRUTH as an excuse to be unkind and even hateful. If we do discover sin in the life of someone else it should force us to our knees to pray, not on our toes to expose. If we still feel the need to talk about another person there is one final test.

---

[39] http://www.catholicherald.com/Opinions/

- **IS IT NECESSARY?** Does this need to be said? As our communications lurch forward at reckless speed and it becomes commonplace to tweet, share and blog every time we suspect someone of secret activities, we have to be intentionally taught the value of silence. Does what I'm going to share contribute to the holiness and happiness of our community? In a big, busy family, quiet is a valuable thing.

It's a simple three-fold filter: true, kind and necessary. The people who use it are happier, and the people who live with the people who use it are cradled in grace-filled communication. Remember, what you say about others says more about you than about them.

HOWLING WITH WOLVES OR FLYING WITH EAGLES

Perhaps the most comprehensive conclusion to expanding our social capacity is the words of Colin Powell, 65th United States Secretary of State and a retired four-star general in the United States Army. He wrote the following on the company we keep[40]:

"The less you associate with some people, the more your life will improve. Any time you tolerate mediocrity in others, it increases your mediocrity. An important attribute in successful people is their impatience with negative thinking and negative acting people. As you grow, your associates will change. Some of your friends will not want you to go on. They will want you to stay where they are. Friends that don't help you climb will want you to crawl. Your friends will stretch your vision or choke your dream. Those that don't increase you will eventually decrease you.

"Consider this: Never receive counsel from unproductive people. Never discuss your problems with someone incapable of contributing to the solution, because those who never succeed themselves are always first to tell you how. Not everyone has a right to speak into your life. You are certain

[40] https://www.goodreads.com/quotes/310930-the-less-you-associate-with-some-people-the-more-your

to get the worst of the bargain when you exchange ideas with the wrong person. Don't follow anyone who's not going anywhere.

"With some people you spend an evening: with others you invest it. Be careful where you stop to inquire for directions along the road of life. Wise is the person who fortifies his life with the right friendships. If you run with wolves, you will learn how to howl. But, if you associate with eagles, you will learn how to soar to great heights.

"A mirror reflects a man's face, but what he is really like is shown by the kind of friends he chooses. The simple but true fact of life is that you become like those with whom you closely associate - for the good and the bad.

"Be not mistaken. This is applicable to family as well as friends. Yes...do love, appreciate and be thankful for your family, for they will always be your family no matter what. Just know that they are human first and though they are family to you, they may be a friend to someone else and will fit somewhere in the criteria above. Never make someone a priority when you are only an option for them."

Amazingly, once we start building our social capacity we will soon discover the need to build our intellectual capacity.

CHAPTER 4
Intellectual Capacity
We need to swop our shoes

The true sign of maturity is being big enough to say, "I was wrong", and even though it might take courage to stand up for what's right, it takes even more to do it in love. Once we have befriended people from different communities we will need to start opening our hearts and our minds to think this way. There must be an expansion of our INTELLECTUAL CAPACITY if we want to grow and mature as believers.

Let's be honest, it has become quite an accolade within certain Christian circles to declare that *"I am a Christian fundamentalist!"* Proclaiming that *"I am not ashamed to stand for the truth"* has become quite popular in recent times. It seems we have fallen into the insular trap of accepted, collective thinking. We live among those who think like us, look like us, talk like us, and we assure ourselves we are right and others are wrong. I have even seen some Facebook pages which boldly announce the following on the cover photo: *"WARNING: If you don't like hearing about Jesus Christ then you've chosen the wrong friend."* This is so unbiblical if we consider Jesus. He always hung out with those who made the religious — those who insisted on being right and defending their religion — uncomfortable. Whether it was prostitutes, tax collectors or "sinners" Jesus was often in their midst. If Jesus had a Facebook page it would probably read as follows: *"WELCOME: If you don't like hearing about religion then you've chosen the right friend."*

One of the main misconceptions of "radical Christians" is being a fundamentalist in the LITERAL WORD but showing contempt for the LIVING WORD, the heart of Christ.

The Center for Action and Contemplation[41] provides the following definition of a fundamentalist:

"Fundamentalism is a growing phenomenon, not only in Islam and other religions, but within Christianity as well. Fundamentalism refuses to listen to the deep levels of mythic, metaphorical, and mystical meaning. It is obsessed with literalism and exclusion. The egoic need for clarity and certitude leads fundamentalists to use sacred writings in a mechanical, closed-ended, and quite authoritarian manner. The ego rarely asks real questions and mostly gives quick answers. This invariably leaves ego-driven, fundamentalist minds and groups utterly trapped in their own cultural moment in history. Thus they miss the Gospel's liberating message along with the deepest challenges and consolations of Scripture.

"Evil gains its power from disguise. Jesus undid the mask of disguise and revealed that our true loyalty was seldom really to God, but to power, money, and group belonging. (In fact, religion is often the easiest place to hide from God.)

"The final and full Word of God is that spiritual authority lies not just in ancient texts but in the living Christ of history, church, community, creation, and our own experience confirming its truth. The mystery is "Christ among you, your hope of glory" (Colossians 1:27)—this is the living Bible! Keep one foot in both camps—the historical text and the present moment. Words are fingers pointing to the moon, but words are never the moon itself. Not knowing this has kept much religion infantile, arrogant, and even dangerous."

I, for one, have a tendency to have deaf ears to arguments that oppose my convictions. But it is mostly my opposition that sees the "blind spots" in my arguments and the flaws in my fundamentalism. Over the years I have seen my own interpretations of Scripture change and mature. Scripture has not changed, but my field of experience and Biblical and cultural

---

[41] https://cac.org/

understandings have. If I had the ability earlier in my Christian life to understand that I could be wrong, the process of maturity could have been so much easier and so much faster.

I have come to an understanding that one of the corner stones in building intellectual capacity is remembering these four powerful words in our conversations: *"I could be wrong..."* Always begin a discussion of importance with the following simple line: *"I want to share my conviction, but I could be wrong ..."*

F. Scott Fitzgerald said, *"The test of a first-rate intelligence is the ability to hold two opposed ideas in mind at the same time and still retain the ability to function."* To which I would add that *the test of an expanded capacity is the ability to hold two opposed convictions in mind at the same time and still retain the ability to hold on to your own.*

PLANK EYE DISEASE

According to Jesus, the true mark of a hypocrite is someone who is so busy finding fault with others that they are completely blind to their own faults[42]. A question we as Christians need to ask ourselves is why we believe what we believe and why do we always believe we are right, even when we are wrong? Why is it so difficult to look at our own convictions from another perspective and to step into someone else's shoes and look from their point of view?

The reason is simple: we do not always infuse our theology with a deep and continued sense of self-examination. Making excuses is far easier than forgiving and rationalising hatred and prejudice far easier than seeking reconciliation. These attitudes are as old as creation. In fact, we can trace this habit all the way back to the Garden of Eden. For when God asked Adam

---

[42] Matthew 7:3-5 "Why do you look at the speck of sawdust in your brother's eye and pay no attention to the plank in your own eye? How can you say to your brother, 'Let me take the speck out of your eye,' when all the time there is a plank in your own eye? You hypocrite, first take the plank out of your own eye, and then you will see clearly to remove the speck from your brother's eye.

if he had eaten of the tree he was commanded not to, Adam created the world's first excuse, *"the woman you put here with me — she gave me some fruit from the tree, and I ate it*." (Genesis 3:12) And when God asked Eve what she had done, she gave the world's second excuse, "*The serpent deceived me, and I ate."* (Genesis 3:13)

Sadly, Christians are often notorious for an emotional kind of terrorism, judgmental attitudes and spiteful comments. Just visit Google and type in the name of any prominent Christian leader. The praise and criticism from anybody with an opinion can be equally overwhelming. Some of the emails we receive at INcontext are sometimes just downright mean.   Jesus addressed this issue in a very uncompromising way in Matthew 7:3-5 *"Why do you look at the speck of sawdust in your brother's eye and pay no attention to the plank in your own eye? How can you say to your brother, 'Let me take the speck out of your eye,' when all the time there is a plank in your own eye? You hypocrite, first take the plank out of your own eye, and then you will see clearly to remove the speck from your brother's eye."*

Why is it so easy to point fingers, to find excuses and to spot the sawdust in the eye of our neighbours? There are numerous contributing factors to this. Jeremy Myers, in an article **FREEDOM FROM RELIGION**, writes the following on Reasons why Christians are mean[43]:

"Some of it is our theology. Many Christians develop a sense of entitlement because we are the "chosen ones" the "elite" the members of the family of God. We feel this gives us the right to look down upon others who are not one of us.

"Sometimes, our behaviour is a result of our understanding of God's grace and forgiveness. We feel that because God forgives us for all our sins, we can treat others in terrible ways, and God will still forgive us. His grace is never a license to treat others so shamefully.

---

[43] https://redeeminggod.com/10-excuses-christians-give-for-treating-others-badly/

"Then there is the critical, judgmental legalistic attitude so often taught and practiced in churches. Since we feel we have a corner on the truth and that we are the ones who are always right, this makes us believe that it is our responsibility to be the world's policemen, going around pointing out where people are wrong and how they are sinning. This is rarely received well by anyone, especially when we have glaringly obvious sins in our own life.

"Finally, there is the fact that Christians love to pick and choose which sins are the worst – things like homosexuality and abortion – while ignoring sins that are prevalent within our own congregations (which might actually be much worse) – sins like gluttony, greed, and pride. The watching world sees our blatant hypocrisy and criticizes us in return for our unjustified criticism of them."

This "plank eye" disease is one of the major obstacles when pursuing an expansion in our intellectual capacity. And this is not questioning our God-view according to what Scripture teaches us but our world-view according to what others teach us.

Faith TV, YouTube and Facebook have in a sense created lazy Christians. It has become a lot easier to find people we agree with and adopt their convictions, rather than struggling with the issues ourselves. So we let some brilliant person struggle with the issues and then accept whatever she or he says.

Few people have the ability to argue for a point that they disagree with. As a matter of fact, I have met few Christians in my nearly forty years of ministry that have mastered the art of shoe-swopping when it comes to theological convictions. Shoe-swopping, the ability to put yourself in the other person's shoes, is a fundamental component in capacity growth. It's almost as magical as shape-swopping in sci-fi fantasy. It's the scientific method applied to the intellect.

We will only expand our capacity once we place ourselves, our theologies, our convictions and our world-views in someone else's shoes and observe our position from their perspective. This does not mean we compromise our convictions by adopting other convictions but it does mean we affirm our conviction by understanding the reasoning behind other convictions.

Easier said than done!

The challenge of shoe-swopping is not only getting into another pair of shoes and swopping our views, it is the fact that we must get out of our own shoes first. Our intellect is often clouded by the fact that we see ourselves superior in knowledge to most people we encounter. We always refer to Jesus rebuking the Pharisees, but we never recognise the Pharisee in our own hearts.

One of the dangers of shoe-swopping is that we run the risk of seeing ourselves as others would see us—not quite as smart as we think. But the pay-offs are worth it.

Grand though in theory, the challenge is in the practical details. Most of us think we're already great listeners and fabulous empathizers, but thinking it doesn't make it so.

SOLDIERS OR SCOUTS

The questions we need to ask ourselves in this regard, says decision-making expert **Julia Galef** at a recent **TED** forum[44] is whether we are SOLDIERS or SCOUTS? The answer to this question, according to Galef, could determine how clearly we see the world. She elaborates as follows:

*"Imagine for a moment you're a **SOLDIER** in the heat of battle — perhaps a Roman foot soldier, medieval archer or Zulu warrior. Regardless of your time and place, some things are probably constant. Your adrenaline is elevated, and your actions stem from your deeply ingrained reflexes, reflexes that are rooted in a need to protect yourself and your side and to defeat the enemy.*

---

*"Now, try to imagine playing a very different role: the **SCOUT**. The scout's job is not to attack or defend; it's to understand. The scout is the one going out, mapping the terrain, identifying potential obstacles. Above all, the scout wants to know what's really out there as accurately as possible. In an actual army, both the soldier and the scout are essential.*

"You can also think of the SOLDIER and SCOUT roles as mindsets — metaphors for how all of us process information and ideas in our daily lives. Having good judgment and making good decisions, it turns out, depends largely about which mindset you're in. We often view information that differs from our convictions as "the enemy", and we want to shoot them down and defend our own opinions.

*"So, the question arises: What does it say about the human mind that we can find such paltry evidence to be compelling enough to convict a man? This is a case of what scientists refer to as "**motivated reasoning,**" a phenomenon in which our unconscious motivations, desires and fears shape the way we interpret information. Some pieces of information feel like our allies — we want them to win; we want to defend them. And other pieces of information are the enemy, and we want to shoot them down. That's why Gale calls motivated reasoning a "**SOLDIER MINDSET."***

Galef points to experiences we can all identify with. When following one of our favourite teams in a specific sport, as an example, and the referee judges that our team has committed a foul, we're probably highly motivated to find reasons why he's wrong. But if he judges that the other team committed a foul — that's a good call. Or, maybe we've read an article or a study that examined a controversial policy, like the much-debated gun control in the USA. As researchers have demonstrated, if we support gun control and the study shows it's not effective, then we're highly motivated to point out all the reasons why the study was poorly designed. But if it shows that gun control works, it's a good study. And vice versa.

Our judgment is strongly influenced, unconsciously, by which side we want to win — and this is universal. This shapes how we think about our health, our relationships, how we decide how to vote, and what we consider fair or ethical. What's most concerning about **motivated reasoning** or the **SOLDIER MINDSET** is just how unconscious it is. We can think we're being objective and fair-minded and still wind up breaking relationships along the way.

What mature Christianity represents is what Galef calls a *"SCOUT MINDSET"*, the drive not to make one idea win or another lose, but to see what's there as honestly and accurately as we can, even if it's not pretty, convenient or pleasant. Galef has spent the last few years examining a **SCOUT MINDSET** and figuring out why some people, at least sometimes, seem able to cut through their own prejudices, biases and motivations and attempt to see the facts and the evidence as objectively as they can. The answer, she found, is emotional. **SCOUT MINDSET** means seeing what's there as accurately as you can, even if it's not pleasant.

Galef explains: *"Just as **SOLDIER MINDSET** is rooted in emotional responses, **SCOUT MINDSET** is too — but it's simply rooted in different emotions. For example, scouts are curious. They're more likely to say they feel pleasure when they learn new information or solve a puzzle. They're more likely to feel intrigued when they encounter something that contradicts their expectations. SCOUTS also have different values. They're more likely to say they think it's virtuous to test their own beliefs, and they're less likely to say that someone who changes their mind seems weak. And, above all, SCOUTS are grounded, which means their self-worth as a person isn't tied to how right or wrong they are about any topic. For example, they can believe that gun control works and if studies come out that show it doesn't, they can say, "Looks like I might be wrong. Doesn't mean I'm bad or stupid." This cluster of traits is what researchers have found — and Galef found anecdotally — predicts good judgment."*

The key takeaway about the traits associated with a SCOUT mindset is they have little to do with how smart you are or how much you know. They don't correlate very closely to IQ at all; they're about how you feel. Galef refers to a particular quote from Antoine de Saint-Exupéry, author of The Little

Prince. *"If you want to build a ship, don't drum up your men to collect wood and give orders and distribute the work,"* he said. *"Instead, teach them to yearn for the vast and endless sea."*

In other words, if we really want to improve our judgment as individuals and as societies, what we need most is not more instruction in logic, rhetoric, probability or economics, even though those things are all valuable. What we most need to use those principles well is to expand a **SCOUT MINDSET**. We need to change the way we feel — to learn how to feel proud instead of ashamed when we notice we might have been wrong about something, or to learn how to feel intrigued instead of defensive when we encounter some information that contradicts our beliefs.

So, the question we need to consider is: What do we most yearn for — to defend our own beliefs or to see the world as clearly as we possibly can? This is, in a nutshell, what ultimately will determine whether we expand or decrease our intellectual capacity. There will be no neutral ground.

A point in case is the Rohingya refugees. Since September 2017 more than **600,000 Rohingya refugees** fled into Bangladesh due to violence in Myanmar. The Rohingya crisis has left at least **1,000 people dead**, including children and infants. Dozens drowned when their overloaded boats capsized in rough waters. The Rohingya people group is the biggest persecuted minority in the world and also one of the least reached people groups in the world being 100% Muslim and with 0.0 % Christians. The scenes of hopelessness and fear of refugees seeking shelter with no resources, no covering and no food were heart-breaking.

However, during the hopelessness of the situation, very few Christians spoke up for the persecuted group, forgotten by most of the Western world.

At a seminar I presented after the news broke of the crisis in Myanmar, there was the normal Q&A time at the end of the conference and the first question asked was the familiar one I hear at every seminar I present. *"Why*

*don't the secular media report on the persecution of Christians?" "Let me
ask the same question but from another perspective," I answered. "Why do
Christians only pray for the persecuted Church and have so little concern for
other minorities who are persecuted?"*

There was an uncomfortable silence. Christians often act as if persecution
is the only mark of authentic Christianity and that the Lord favours only
those believers who have endured suffering. But this theology has
misplaced God's character into a dogma that was created by a small-
capacity-Christianity. You see, God's concern is not persecution per se, but
injustice. There is no doubt that the Lord honours those who face injustice
for His name's sake[45] but because God is a God of love His pursuit of justice
extends far beyond the Christian community. God is bigger than just
Christianity. He not only cares about injustice against those who follow Him
but injustice against all, in every community and as a principle for all
humanity.

Christians should scout and not defend. We should be concerned about the
injustice against any group of people, regardless of race, culture, religion or
orientation. We need to place ourselves in the shoes of those who are
different from us. We need to pursue an expansion of our intellectual
capacity in the following ways:

1. By being readers
2. By being researchers
3. By being receivers
4. By being reshapeable

SCOUTS ARE READERS

The average CEO reads 60 books a year. Why? Because they know that the
key to success is constant learning.

---

[45] Matthew 5:11 "Blessed are you when people insult you, persecute you and falsely say all kinds of
evil against you because of me.

If we are truly serious about expanding our intellectual capacity we need to make a case for reading widely, generously and intelligently. It is unfortunate if we read only the material we already like and research only the facts that confirm what we already believe. If we never stretch ourselves to engage authors that we may be inclined to disagree with, we never experience the richness of expanding our intellectual capacity.

Leaders are readers. This is not only a nice quote but a proven scientific fact. If we want to expand our intellectual capacity we will have to return to the old habit of picking up a book and reading it. For thousands of years, stories have been told through the pages of a book. But with the advent of new technologies, the ways humans communicate their teachings, sermons, memories, discoveries and life lessons have increasingly been captured and retold through a new variety of media. The challenge in the modern-day Church is that we have generally become junk-food believers with short inspirational video messages being the main course on the menu. We have lost the ability to digest the solid food of well-written books by heroes of faith from years gone by.

In a report on Medical daily[46], detailed research shows how watching videos and TV changes neural pathways, as opposed to reading a book. The conclusion in the research shows that watching television can change the way the human brain makes connections, while books enhance neural pathways.

In 2013, a team of researchers from Ohio State University interviewed and tested pre-schoolers and their parents to see how television impacted a child's theory of mind. Ultimately, it was found that if the television was on near the child, even if they were not watching it, it impaired their theory of mind, which is defined as the ability to recognize their own and another person's beliefs, intents, desires, and knowledge.

---

[46] http://www.medicaldaily.com/neural-pathways-watching-tv-human-brain-reading-book-389744

The research also shows that reading strengthens the neural pathways like any muscle in your body. Even at a young age, children who are read to by their parents develop five enhanced reading skills, which include an advanced vocabulary, word recognition in spoken words, ability to connect written letters to spoken sounds, reading comprehension, and the fluency to read text accurately and quickly.

Gregory Berns, director of Emory's Center for Neuropolicy, reported in a statement: *"We already knew that good stories can put you in someone else's shoes in a figurative sense. Now we're seeing that something may also be happening biologically."*

To build intellectual capacity the solution is simple: READ MORE, WATCH LESS.

SCOUTS ARE RESEARCHERS

Being informed is not always about getting the right answers, it's about asking the right questions. Scouts ask questions that will challenge their personal convictions and not necessarily confirm them. If we want to expand our intellectual capacity we will have to invest time and effort into seeking explanation before sensation. This is probably one of the greatest challenges in Christian circles today.

The story in John 20:25 of Thomas who did not believe the apostles when they told him that "they have seen the Lord," gave him the nickname of Thomas the *DOUBTER*. I believe the nickname should have been Thomas the *RESEARCHER*. His concerns were legitimate, and his request was sound: *"Unless I see the nail marks in his hands and put my finger where the nails were, and put my hand into his side, I will not believe."*[47]

---

[47] John 20:25 So the other disciples told him, "We have seen the Lord!" But he said to them, "Unless I see the nail marks in his hands and put my finger where the nails were, and put my hand into his side, I will not believe."

With all the fake news bombarding Christian media today and all the false prophets flooding our pulpits, we need more followers of Christ with the mentality of Thomas: People who will seek the marks of the cross; forgiveness, reconciliation and redemption, before simply passing on any information as truth.

In his book T*he rise of political lying*[48] Peter Osborne, a leading political journalist, asks the question *"is it now time to question the creeping invasion of falsehood?"* Peter suggests that we now live in a "post truth" environment where *"public statements are no longer fact based but ... are constructed to serve a purpose"*. That is exactly what we are seeing with the rise of fake news.

Sadly, the Christian media have not escaped this deceitful practice. We often find messages on social media that call on Christians to pray for events that never occurred (*the 20 churches that have supposedly been burnt down by Buddhist extremists in the Indian province of Olisabang*[49]) or events that happened years ago (*the capture of the Christian town of Qaraqosh in Syria by Islamic state*[50]). There are also countless stories that have been deliberately exaggerated (*the report of ISIS camps being established in South Africa*[51]) or designed specifically to deceive and manipulate Christians with a specific agenda (*arms seized en route to refugee camps*[52]). Often stories are motivated by sincere prayers for the persecuted Church (*violent murder of woman in Syria*[53] or *Christians burnt in Nigeria*[54]) or even attempts to share stories of

---

[48] https://www.amazon.co.uk/Rise Political-Lying-Peter-Oborne/dp/0743275608
[49] http://www.incontextinternational.org/2016/10/01/churches-burned-down-and-christians-targeted-in-india/
[50] http://www.incontextinternational.org/2016/10/23/urgent-call-for-prayer-for-queragosh/
[51] http://www.incontextinternational.org/2016/10/23/muslims-buying-up-farms-in-petrusville-south-africa/
[52] http://www.incontextinternational.org/2016/10/23/arms-seized-en-route-to-refugee-camps/
[53] http://www.incontextinternational.org/2016/10/23/email-about-murdered-syrian-woman/
[54] http://www.incontextinternational.org/2016/10/23/reports-of-christians-burnt-in-nigeria/

miracles (*ISIS fighter converts to Christianity*). Sadly many of these stories are often based on deliberate lies, intentional satire or selective disinformation.

What we mostly suffer from in this age of information is not over-exposure but filter-failure. For Christians the challenge is to use Biblical filters when surfing through the internet, common sense when reading articles and discernment before forwarding or posting them. It has become far too easy to like, copy, paste and distribute negative reports that serve a specific racial or political agenda in making a point. It has become equally easy to simply post links to videos that confirm, explore and feed on our fears and prejudices. Enemies are created every day by well-meaning believers who proudly call themselves "Watchmen on the wall" who, in the name of truth, often see opportunities as enemies and interpret God-at-work as the enemy-at-work.

As Christians we desperately need to embrace a culture of research before believing anything that bears the name of Jesus, and to draw the line when information contradicts the radical call of a Saviour who called His followers to BE different in order to offer the world an alternative spirit to hatred, fear, suspicion, and division.

Here are 6 guidelines to follow in our endeavours to be true scouts and Christians who seek to expand our intellectual capacity by researching well. When reading or posting an article, first determine the following:

1. Does it encourage reconciliation or division?

2 Corinthians 5:18-19 All this is from God, who reconciled us to himself through Christ and gave us the ministry of reconciliation: that God was reconciling the world to himself in Christ, not counting people's sins against them. And he has committed to us the message of reconciliation.

Messages that create content that polarizes communities should always be viewed with suspicion. People long to belong. Unless we provide a platform where strangers and enemies can become family and friends we are no better than the world. When people are polarized they find alternative groups to belong to. By passing on messages of division we are playing into the hands of the enemy and promoting exactly the same cause that we aim to fight.

2. Does it give life or drain life?
Proverbs 18:21 The tongue has the power of life and death, and those who love it will eat its fruit.

There is no neutral exchange in communication: messages either give life or drain life. Christians are called to:
- Communicate **LIFE**: *Proverbs 10:11 The mouth of the righteous is a fountain of life, but the mouth of the wicked conceals violence.*
- Communicate **RIGHTEOUSNESS**: *Psalm 35:28 My tongue will proclaim your righteousness, your praises all day long.*
- Communicate **WISDOM:** *Proverbs 10:31 From the mouth of the righteous comes the fruit of wisdom, but a perverse tongue will be silenced.*
- Communicate **HEALING**: *Proverbs 12:18 The words of the reckless pierce like swords, but the tongue of the wise brings healing.*
- Communicate **ENCOURAGEMENT:** *Isaiah 50:4 The LORD has given me a well-instructed tongue, to know the word that sustains the weary.*
- Communicate **UNDERSTANDING**: *Proverbs 2:6 For the LORD gives wisdom; from his mouth come knowledge and understanding.*
- Communicate **JUSTICE**: *Proverbs 8:8 All the words of my mouth are just; none of them is crooked or perverse.*
- Communicate **TRUTH:** *Proverbs 8:7 My mouth speaks what is true, for my lips detest wickedness.*
- Communicate with **CARE**: *Ecclesiastes 5:2 Do not be quick with your mouth, ... so let your words be few.*

Yes indeed, (1Peter 3:10) for, "*Whoever would love life and see good days must keep their tongue from evil and their lips from deceitful speech.*"

3. Does it provide hope or create fear?

2Timothy 1:7 For God hath not given us the spirit of fear; but of power, and of love, and of a sound mind.

Messages that create fear or anger in the heart of the reader should be avoided at all costs. Fear paralyses and never leads to an anguish for the lost. Always investigate the heart behind any communication. Any message which creates fear should be seen as a message from the enemy and not from the Lord. Rather than slamming the negatives of religions, races, people and political parties, we have to provide alternative messages of hope if we aim to change hearts, perception and mindsets.

4. Does it inspire love or hatred?

Luke 6:27 But to you who are listening I say: "Love your enemies, do good to those who hate you."

Messages that are based on bias and that lead to an "us and them" mentality should be avoided at all costs. The post-modern world has become a global village divided by "us" and "them", whether it be "them" the refugees, "them" the Muslims, "them" who are culturally/ religiously/ racially different from us, or simply "them" — those who do not fit into my box, defined by my cultural worldviews. Sadly, Christians often view the "unknown" from a safe haven, snugly positioned into the "us" box. "Them" the sinners, "them" the unsaved or simply "them" the non-Christians give us a moral system to fall back on that which distinguishes "us" from "them".

Hatred in any form, even in the name of truth, disguised in any way, should always raise red flags.

5. Does it gather or scatter?

Matthew 12:30 Whoever is not with me is against me, and whoever does not gather with me scatters.

Messages that are not focused on redemptive purposes, the gathering of souls, should be ignored. Every follower of Christ has a mandate to seek redemptive purposes in all communication, whether an email, a WhatsApp, on Facebook or simply a comment on the internet. For Christians there is no neutral ground – we either gather or we scatter. Any messages that focus on the danger, the threat or the menace of another group are messages that scatter, even though the intent might be noble.

6. Does it stimulate peace or conflict?
James 3:18 Peacemakers who sow in peace reap a harvest of righteousness.

Messages that stimulate conflict always run the risk of destroying any work that might be in progress. In the times we live in it is easy to stimulate anger and establish conflict. We live in angry societies and the smallest spark can start a revolution. As Christians we have a mandate to use our communication, verbal or written, as ways of establishing peace. If not, we have nothing to offer.

Here are a further 6 Guidelines before believing any articles[55]

1. Be sceptical.
There's an old saying in journalism: "If your mother says she loves you, check it out." Reporters are supposed to look hard at what they think they know, and so should their audience. Reputable news outlets "show their work", so you can see how they came to their conclusions. Are the sources solid? Does the logic makes sense?

2. If the story is sensational, be more sceptical.
Amazing things are amazing for a reason: they don't happen very often. There are a lot more amazing stories in the world — because they make money — than there are amazing things that actually happened. This is why serious news sources tend to be less exciting to read than tabloids are. Memorize or bookmark these fact-checking sites: www.Politifact.com, www.Factcheck.org, www.Washington Post Factchecker, www.Snopes.com

---

[55] http://www.huffingtonpost.com/entry/use-these-7-tips-to-tell-real-news-from-fake_us_58a4dbf8e4b0b0e1e0e2064b

3. If the story reinforces what you already believe, be even more sceptical.

We all suffer from confirmation bias, the tendency to accept information that supports our beliefs, and ignore or reject information that doesn't. If you want accurate information instead of just flattery, you're going to have to fight your own confirmation bias. And please, don't fall into the trap of assuming that all news you don't like is "fake".

4. Check the sources.

The sources of a story are like the foundation of a building: if they're not solid, the whole thing is likely to collapse. Sources should be objective and as close to the original information as possible. So, for example, a respected, independent scientific research organization is more credible than a partisan think tank, and still more credible than a random person with an opinion.

There should also be more than one source, unless the story is an interview or there is something exceptional about what this source has to say. Beware of attempts to fool you with sources that look credible, but aren't. These include organizations that appear to be government agencies, respected research institutions, or major news organizations, but aren't. Look them up. While even the best sources can make mistakes, there's usually a good reason for a good reputation.

5. Check the logic.

Not only should the facts of the story be solid, so should the way they're connected. Let's say you hear that a person wearing sneakers has robbed a bank. Does this mean all sneaker-wearers are probably bank robbers? Of course not. If a scientific study found that many bank robbers do wear sneakers, then we'd at least know there's a correlation of some kind. But we still wouldn't know that wearing sneakers means someone is likely to be a crook. It could just be that robbers like to be able to run fast. All of this would need to be checked out.

It may be easy to see the problem with jumping to conclusions about sneaker wearers, but this kind of illogic is common in less-than-credible news outlets, and often goes unchallenged by consumers. For example, because some immigrants commit crimes, many people conclude that immigrants are more dangerous, and some news outlets encourage that belief. But the logic doesn't follow, and when we check the facts, we find that first generation immigrants commit less crime than native-born citizens do.

6. Understand what you're looking at.

The difference between reliable and unreliable isn't always black and white. There are different kinds of content that meet, or fail to meet, different kinds of standards:

- **Hard news**. This is just the facts. For example: "A home on 13th St. suffered extensive damage last night after a 30-foot elm tree was blown over by 60 mph winds."
- **Opinion.** This may be an editorial, an op-ed (in newspapers, this is opinion that appears on the page opposite the editorial page), or a blog post. It's not a problem if it's biased — that's what opinion means. Many good newspapers have a clear bias on their editorial pages, but give straight reporting on their news pages. Reputable opinion writers will base their arguments on verifiable facts, because opinion isn't an excuse to make things up.
- **Feature story**. This is softer, interpretive coverage of a story or people, exploring meaning and emotion.
- **Biased, but still valid, news**. Since reporters are humans, it's impossible for any of them to be 100 percent bias free As long as they're careful with facts and logic, such outlets can be worth consulting — especially if they challenge your own biases.
- **News that's so biased it's misleading.** To support their in-house bias, some outlets twist facts and logic so much that they do more harm than good. This describes some tabloids.
- **Fake news**. Fake news is just made up from thin air.

SCOUTS ARE RECEIVERS

The only way we will ever effectively "swop shoes" and understand the opinions and convictions of others will not only be through effective communication but especially through effective listening. We need to be able to receive information before imparting information and this is probably the main obstacle in any process of reconciliation. We are eager to share and convict but hesitant to receive and accept. Effective listening is a skill that requires nurturing and needs development.

Coaching for Change[56] provides the following different levels of listening:

Level 1 Listening:
When we are listening at level 1 the focus of our attention is on how the words the other person is saying affect us with minimal concern for the person talking. The attention is on me — what are my thoughts, judgments, issues, conclusions and feelings. There is no room to let in the feelings of the person being "listened" to. When listening at level 1 our opinions and judgments arise. Level 1 listening is appropriate when you are gathering information for yourself like getting directions or ordering in a restaurant or a store.

Level 2 Listening:
When we listen at level 2, there is a deeper focus on the person being listened to. This often means not even being aware of the context. Our awareness is totally on the other person. We notice what they say as well as how they say it and what they don't say. We listen for what they value and what is important to them. We listen for what gives them energy or sadness or resignation. We let go of judgment. We are no longer planning what we are going to say next. We respond to what we actually hear.

---

[56] https://www.coachingforchange.com/pub10.html

Level 3 Listening:

When we listen more deeply than the two levels described above, in addition to the conversation we take in all information that surrounds the conversation. We are aware of the context and the impact of the context on all parties. We include all our senses, in particular our intuition. We consider what is not being said and we notice the energy in the room and in the person we are listening to. We use that information to ask more effective questions.

SCOUTS ARE RESHAPABLE

The process of reading, researching and recollecting will require an open mind and an open Bible.

There is an old missional saying that states, "if your vision doesn't scare you, it is probably not from the Lord". The visions that God gives us are mostly far beyond our current capacity; which allows us to grow into them and also to grow into faith. But too often, our capacity building process is limited or aborted not because of a lack of faith but because of a lack of flexibility.

Peter's experience in Acts 10:9-17[57] is a perfect example. The Lord provides a magnificent opportunity for Peter to expand his capacity as an apostle by taking the gospel outside the Jewish nation to someone "uncultural, untraditional and unclean" to be ministered to. But Peter is limited by his rigid theology and insists on following the Jewish ceremonial law. After all, this is what Scripture commands, is it not? As God speaks to Peter in this "uncultural" vision, Peter realises that a new assignment often requires a new approach. You can't fulfil a dream with the same capacity you had

---

[57] Acts 10:9-14 About noon the following day as they were on their journey and approaching the city, Peter went up on the roof to pray. He became hungry and wanted something to eat, and while the meal was being prepared, he fell into a trance. He saw heaven opened and something like a large sheet being let down to earth by its four corners. It contained all kinds of four-footed animals, as well as reptiles and birds. Then a voice told him, "Get up, Peter. Kill and eat." "Surely not, Lord!" Peter replied. "I have never eaten anything impure or unclean."

when you received it. You need to grow, build and develop a bigger capacity. And you cannot develop capacity if you're not flexible.

In Luke 5:33-38[58] Jesus answers the Pharisees on a question, probably more an accusation, about fasting and feasting. They say to him, *"John's disciples often fast and pray, and so do the disciples of the Pharisees, but yours go on eating and drinking."* (33)

This accusation was not so much about the feasting but about the disciples' inability to observe their religious duties. Jesus then answers them with a parable about a wineskin: *"No one pours new wine into old wineskins. Otherwise, the new wine will burst the skins; the wine will run out and the wineskins will be ruined."* This answer was a convicting reminder that the inability to be reshapable will limit capacity and ultimately lead to religious inertia[59]

Hastings *Dictionary of Christ and the Gospels*[60] summarises the context of this parable as follows:
"In ancient Israel, the grapes were pressed in the winepress and left in the collection vats for a few days. Fermentation starts immediately on pressing, and this allows the first "tumultuous" (gassy) phase to pass. Then the fermenting juice was put in clay jars to be stored, or into wineskins if it was to be transported some distance.

"The wineskins were partially tanned goat skins, sewn at the holes where the leg and tail had been. The skins were filled with the partially fermented wine in the opening at the neck and then tied it off. If one puts freshly pressed fermenting juice directly into the skin and close it off, the tumultuous stage of fermentation would burst the wineskins, but after this

---

[58] Luke 5:37 -38 And no one pours new wine into old wineskins. Otherwise, the new wine will burst the skins; the wine will run out and the wineskins will be ruined. No, new wine must be poured into new wineskins.

[59] a property of matter by which it remains at rest or in uniform motion in the same straight line unless acted upon by some external force

[60] http://www.ccel.org/ccel/hastings/dict2/Page_824.html

stage, the skins have enough stretchiness to handle the rest of the fermentation process. However, skins that have already been used and stretched out ("old wineskins") cannot be used again since they cannot stretch again. If they are used again for holding wine that is still in the process of fermenting ("new wine"), they will burst. A similar thing happens today when a balloon is blown up past its ability to contain the air inside, and "pop", it bursts."

This parable is as much about being able to progressively and continuously reshape our theology as it is about building and developing our capacity. Those who follow Christ must not only be open to learning new values and new principles, they must be expectant of it and prepare accordingly. The Gospel of the Kingdom and transformation which Jesus preached, lived and demanded, could not fit into the Pharisees' paradigm or way of living because of a lack of flexibility and a lack of capacity. They were religious, pious and virtuous but they lacked the ability to adjust their theology.

Richard Rohr said the following:
"I've come to see that what matters most is not our **STATUS** *but our* **TRAJECTORY**, *not where we are but where we're going, not where we stand but where we're headed. . . . [Religion] is at its best when it leads us forward, when it guides us on our spiritual growth as individuals and in our cultural evolution as a species. Unfortunately, religion often becomes more of a cage than a guide, holding us back rather than summoning."*

This, however, runs parallel with testing Scripture and finding the balance between "new truths" and "old truths", and "new truths" and "new heresies". As William Barclay rightly said: *"We must always have an open mind, but not open on both sides."* The reality is that in building capacity, as we mature on the journey of faith, sometimes some of our belief systems "must change".

Amazingly, once we start building our intellectual capacity we will soon discover the need to build our mental capacity.

CHAPTER 5
Mental Capacity
We need to modify our thinking

The challenge in life is not only to value what we BELIEVE but also what we FEED our belief-system. The mental ability and thought-process by which we form our convictions are often neglected on the journey of faith. There must be an expansion of our **MENTAL CAPACITY** if we want to grow and mature as believers. Expanding our spiritual and intellectual capacity alone could so easily lead to arrogance and an irrelevant faith in a broken world that seeks Truth in the lives of those who confess God, and not in their theory.

The easy solution when we first meet faith is often to settle for quick and easy theologies instead of exploring the depth of God's character and digging deep into scriptures ourselves. The person that introduces us to Christ is normally the person whose convictions we embrace. It is no small matter that 1 Chronicles 22:19 instructs devotees to *"devote their hearts and souls to **SEEKING** the LORD their God"*.

Sadly, Christians often leave their "religious seeking" to pastors, philosophers and prophets. Our understanding then becomes moulded and modelled by the convictions of others and soon our perceptions are shaped by the belief-systems of people we don't even know that well. We follow every Tele-Evangelist, from all spectrums of theology, as infallible men and women of God. We take every word they speak as truth simply because some of the words they speak are true. Their thinking becomes our thinking and soon our mental capacity becomes dependent on others.

We need to expand our thinking and understand that the depth and breadth of our perceptions often determine the depth and breadth of our understanding of God.   Our thoughts need to be aligned not by what man says about God but by what God says about man.

Richard Rohr explains this truth a little easier:
When your small knowing meets God's BIG knowing it's usually a GOOD knowing.

The GOOD KNOWING, and understanding God's BIG KNOWING, is the key in modifying our thinking. This principle cannot be overemphasised. In expanding our mental capacity on our journey of faith it becomes indispensable to feed the soul by exploring the positive while everything around us wants to feed us with the negative. Paul endorses this principle when he speaks to the Church in Philippians (4:8*): "Finally, brothers and sisters, whatever is true, whatever is noble, whatever is right, whatever is pure, whatever is lovely, whatever is admirable—if anything is excellent or praiseworthy—think about such things."*

FEEDING YOUR WOLVES

An old Cherokee legend about a battle between two wolves illustrates the most important battle of our lives — the one between our good and bad thoughts. Here is how the story goes (taken from *Virtues for life*[61]):

An old Cherokee is teaching his grandson about life. "A fight is going on inside me," he said to the boy. *"It is a terrible fight and it is between two wolves. One is evil – he is anger, envy, sorrow, regret, greed, arrogance, self-pity, guilt, resentment, inferiority, lies, false pride, superiority, and ego."* He continued, *"The other is good – he is joy, peace, love, hope, serenity, humility, kindness, benevolence, empathy, generosity, truth, compassion, and faith. The same fight is going on inside you – and inside every other person, too."*

---

[61] https://www.virtuesforlife.com/two-wolves/

The grandson thought about it for a minute and then asked his grandfather, *"Which wolf will win?"* The old Cherokee smiled and simply replied, ***"The one you feed."***

The truth is simple: we will never expand our mental capacity if we feed our souls only with the negative. If we speak only about the negative of our leaders, the corruption in our nations, the evil of other religions and the bad of all that is happening in the world today we disempower the sovereignty of God and nullify the power of the Gospel.

Which wolf will we feed?

When dealing with daily news and the fears, tragedies and disillusions of life, our thoughts can often be our own worst enemy. It never ceases to amaze me how easy it is for our perceptions to create our realities and how deeply dependent our perceptions are on the points of view of other people.

In a latest study by HP Labs[62] it was found that social media, and in particular Facebook, have the power to mess with our ability to think independently. The results show that people were more likely to change their minds about "liking" certain things if enough time had passed and they could see that the other side was even moderately more popular.

In ministry I am often confronted by Christians who choose to "feed" their negativity by feeding themselves on the negativity of others. I receive videos of refugees planning to Islamlse Europe, emails of politicians linked to the anti-Christ, WhatsApp messages focusing on the negative reports of racial conflicts and it seems like there is much joy when negativity gives birth to more negativity and how quickly it turns into a cycle of cynicism.

Richard Rohr explains it as follows: *The world today tends to be cynical about most things. We have a hard time believing in an enchanted world, a*

---

[62] http://mashable.com/2011/09/16/social-media-peer-pressure/#ih.wEBmSbGqz

sacred or benevolent universe. Why would we if we see only at the surface level? Everywhere we turn, every time we watch the news, we see suffering. We have become sceptical about God's goodness, humanity's possibilities, and our planet's future. We can't help seeing what is not and are often unable to recognize or appreciate what is. I see this temptation in myself almost every day. I have to pray and wait for a second gaze, a deeper seeing. This is my daily bread.

Which wolf will we feed?

Joyce Shafer of "selfgrowth"[63] asks the question: *"When negativity knocks at your door, do you recognize it and send it away? Or do you invite it in for dinner, or worse, to stay with you as long as it likes—possibly for your lifetime?"*

Shafer further explains that managing negativity in our lives isn't about the fact we have negative thoughts or feelings—we will. It isn't about eliminating negative thoughts and feelings so that we never experience them again—that's not realistic. It is about training our conscious mind to notice such thoughts and feelings when they appear, and to recognize the different "costumes" negativity wears. The simple reality is that whatever costume negativity puts on, what's really embodied is fear.

Researcher, Dr Elisabeth Kubler-Ross explained that *"Natural anger lasts for only about seventeen seconds. This means the actual emotion you feel (any negative emotion) has its full-charge expression for that period of time. Past that, your conscious (and subconscious) mind takes over, usually engaging in reactions related to whatever fear was triggered."*

The challenge in building a mental capacity that will reflect the consciousness of Christ is quite simple: *__which wolf will we feed?__*

---

[63] http://www.selfgrowth.com/articles/do_you_feed_negativity

THE FIRST CHRISTIAN JOURNALIST

We can build and develop our mental capacity by learning how to discipline our thoughts. We need to approach news with the heart of a journalist that believes that God is still sovereignly in control and not a spectator in global events.

The first Christian "journalist" in Scripture that we read of was Mary Magdalene (John 20:18). She went to investigate the tomb of Jesus and when she found it empty she went to the disciples **WITH THE NEWS**: *"I have seen the Lord!"* There are some valuable lessons to learn from Mary's approach.

This "field report" from Mary is found in John 20:1-12: *Early on the first day of the week, while it was still dark, Mary Magdalene went to the tomb and saw that the stone had been removed from the entrance. So, she came running to Simon Peter and the other disciple, the one Jesus loved, and said, "They have taken the Lord out of the tomb, and we don't know where they have put him!" So, Peter and the other disciple started for the tomb. Both were running, but the other disciple outran Peter and reached the tomb first. He bent over and looked in at the strips of linen lying there but did not go in. Then Simon Peter came along behind him and went straight into the tomb. He saw the strips of linen lying there, as well as the cloth that had been wrapped around Jesus' head. The cloth was still lying in its place, separate from the linen. Finally, the other disciple, who had reached the tomb first, also went inside. He saw and believed. (They still did not understand from Scripture that Jesus had to rise from the dead.) Then the disciples went back to where they were staying. Now Mary stood outside the tomb crying. As she wept, she bent over to look into the tomb and saw two angels in white, seated where Jesus' body had been, one at the head and the other at the foot.*

Can you imagine modern technology being available in those days? Facebook posts, YouTube videos, selfies, WhatsApp messages, Tweets, mobile phone pictures, short-term outreaches and different Christian groups arriving to "catch the fire".

And maybe taking this Scripture as an example of expanding our mental capacity is a little far-fetched, but it does provide a wonderful setting of observing news, putting it into context and then creating a perspective; three elements of expanding our capacity in thinking new.

I love looking beyond the obvious when I read Scripture and look for the specifics in the Bible; verses that could have been omitted that would not have changed the story but were added for a specific reason.
In this Scripture there are three specifics that teach us the principles in expanding our mental capacity:

- The OBSERVATION
- The CONTEXT
- The PERSPECTIVE

OBSERVATION

THE FIRST SPECIFIC IS FOUND IN VERSE 1: **Early** on the first day of the week, **while it was still dark** Mary Magdalene went to the tomb and saw that the stone had been removed from the entrance.

DEFINITION OF OBSERVATION
"The action or process of closely observing or monitoring something or someone. The ability to notice things, especially significant details."

SCRIPTURE TO OBSERVE
Mark 13:28 "Now learn this lesson from the fig tree: As soon as its twigs get tender and its leaves come out, you know that summer is near."

If the Scripture simply read: "On the first day of the week, Mary Magdalene went to the tomb and saw that the stone had been removed from the entrance" we would still have had the essence of the story. But the author added *"Early, when it was still dark."* There was an urgency, no time to be wasted, in the heart of Mary to investigate, and she OBSERVED that the stone had been removed. "Early" refers to an urgency and "while it was still dark" refers to intent. If we seek to expand our mental capacity we need to continually observe with urgency and intent, not curiosity and content. There was both urgency and intent as Mary went first thing, early morning, to inspect the grave. She would not be content to hear later on what happened. She wanted to see for herself.

It is significant to note the different objectives as Mary and the disciples approached and observed the same scene set before them.

Mary came with a sense of urgency, a heart of worship, seeking Christ in the tomb. Peter and John probably came out of curiosity, also with a real sense of urgency (they ran) but, sadly, they looked and went back to where they were staying. Their mental capacity could look at the empty grave and yet not comprehend the significance of what they saw.

It is true that you cannot see what you are not looking for and if you don't get it, you simply don't get it. Those who experience resurrection are those who seek resurrection. Those who seek God in the news of today are those who will find Him. **What we don't pay attention to, we won't see.**

When watching and observing global events it needs to be more than just the curiosity of obtaining information. It's not just considering the cave and having a sensational view of what is presented to us. Truth does not come cheaply. If we truly seek to expand our mental capacity, we should have the clear objective of seeking God in every situation. It's the sacrifice of having a miner mentality and delving deep into what is happening, looking through the redemptive lenses of Christ.

We need to seek Christ when hearing the news of bomb blasts, the updates of disasters, the anguish of wars; in the darkness, in the despair and in the caves of life. We need to separate the noise from the news and not just watch the news but observe the trends and understand the seasons. We need to get the bigger picture with an objective of finding Christ.

In John 12:26 the Lord gives His disciples a very strong indication of how followship should happen. *"Whoever serves me must follow me; and where I am, my servant also will be."*

The challenge within the Christian faith is not only to be equipped to follow Christ according to Scripture but being able to follow Christ according to seasons. We need to watch the news and understand global trends. We need to know "where Christ is" in order to build our mental capacity. I often hear Christians saying to me that they don't watch news anymore because they are overwhelmed by the hopelessness of war, corruption, tragedies and death. Well, have a look in the cave and discover a risen Christ.

When we watch the news without observing God's hand in every event there will no doubt be a sense of hopelessness. When we watch the news with urgency and intent, we will no doubt be struck by an "empty grave" as proof of a risen Christ. But, this will only happen once we discover the context.

CONTEXT

THE SECOND SPECIFIC IS FOUND IN VERSE 7: *The cloth was still lying in its place (wrapped, rolled up, folded), separate from the linen.*

DEFINITION OF CONTEXT
"The circumstances that form the setting for an event, statement, or idea, and in terms of which it can be fully understood."

SCRIPTURE TO CONTEXTUALISE
Mark 13:29 Even so, when you see these things happening, you know that it is near, right at the door.

Once again, we find Mary's approach is completely different from that of the disciples. Mary observes the empty cave with a mental attitude that understands there is something more to discover than just the emptiness. The emptiness excites her as she does not want to miss a thing, even in the unseen. She understands that something significant has taken place and responds by staying behind. Peter and John lack the understanding and fail to interpret the empty cave from a prophetic and Scriptural context. *(John 20:9 They still did not understand from Scripture that Jesus had to rise from the dead.)* The emptiness of the cave disappoints them, and they react by going back home to business as usual.

But the significance of Mary's interpretation of the empty grave probably lies in the cloth, still in its place, separate from the linen (verse 7).

There is a very "romantic" context often used by Western pastors when explaining why Jesus "folded" (not used in all translations) the napkin? But sadly, this theory could be as misleading as it is misinterpreted.

This theory is based on the Hebrew tradition of that day and is as follows: The folded napkin had to do with the Master and Servant, and every Jewish boy knew this tradition. When the servant set the dinner table for the master, he made sure that it was exactly the way the master wanted it. The table was furnished perfectly, and the servant would wait, just out of sight, until the master had finished eating, and would not dare touch that table, until then. Now if the master was done eating, he would rise from the table, wipe his fingers, his mouth, and clean his beard, and would wad up that napkin and toss it onto the table. The servant would then know to clear the table. For in those days, the wadded napkin meant, *"I'm done"*. But if the master got up from the table, and folded his napkin, and laid it beside his plate, the servant would not dare touch the table, because.... the folded napkin meant, *"I'm coming back!"*

For some Western preachers the napkin, or headcloth, being folded separate from the linen is contextually interpreted that Jesus sent this message to His disciples: ***I am coming back!***

But, as nice as this sounds, it remains a nice, romantic, western, misinterpretation of the events. Here is why.

The word "napkin", used in the King James Bible, certainly gives some readers a wrong picture of what was put around the head of Jesus Christ. The Greek word is *"soudarion"*, from a Latin word *"sudarium"*. The cloth is akin to our modern-day handkerchief, though larger in size, like a bandana or a "mitpachat" (head scarves) worn by Jewish women. The word "folded" found in John 20:7 in many Bible translations also gives readers the impression that the "soudarion" was folded like one would fold his handkerchief or a towel.

But the context of the wrapped clothes stretches far deeper than just a sign of Christ's return. The evidence of the intact and not unwrapped grave clothes, both the shroud and the "sudarium" proves that Jesus Christ rose up, from His sleeping position, right though the wrappings, and then passed through the wall of the sepulchre in His resurrected glorified body! This was unlike Lazarus who needed to be loosed from his wrappings after He raised him from the dead (John 11:44[64]).

Here is why the context is important and why this helps us to expand our mental capacity. If we interpret the empty grave and wrapped headscarf as the Lord conveying a message of *"I am coming back"*, then our interpretation will be **PROPHETIC** and focus only on His return. But, if we interpret the empty grave and wrapped headscarf as the Lord conveying a message of *"I am resurrected"*, then our interpretation will be **REDEMPTIVE** and our focus will be on His salvation.

This might seem insignificant at first but will eventually determine how we watch the news, how we interpret disasters, how we view tragedies, how we observe wars and how we contextualize global events. It will prevent us

---

[64] John 11:44 The dead man came out, his hands and feet wrapped with strips of linen, and a cloth around his face. Jesus said to them, "Take off the grave clothes and let him go."

from always seeking the fatalistic **PROPHETIC** approach, and prompt us instead to seek active **REDEMPTIVE** purposes.

To expand our mental capacity will therefore require that we look at world events within a redemptive context that fully comprehends that:

- **God's POWER is sovereign, He is not a spectator.**
  Dan 2:21 He changes times and seasons; he deposes kings and raises up others. He gives wisdom to the wise and knowledge to the discerning.
- **God's PURPOSE is for everybody to be saved.**
  1Ti 2:3 This is good, and pleases God our Saviour, who wants all people to be saved and to come to a knowledge of the truth.
- **God's PRIORITY is His Kingdom, not our comfort.**
  Psalm 145:10-13 All your works praise you, LORD; your faithful people extol you. They tell of the glory of your kingdom and speak of your might, so that all people may know of your mighty acts and the glorious splendor of your kingdom. Your kingdom is an everlasting kingdom, and your dominion endures through all generations. The LORD is trustworthy in all he promises and faithful in all he does.

PERSPECTIVE

THE THIRD SPECIFIC IS FOUND IN VERSE 10: *Then the disciples went back to where they were staying.*

DEFINITION OF PERSPECTIVE
"The appearance of viewed objects with regard to their relative position."
Or *"A particular attitude towards or way of regarding something; a point of view."*

SCRIPTURE TO PLACE EVENTS IN PERSPECTIVE
Mark 13:7 When you hear of wars and rumors of wars, do not be alarmed. Such things must happen, but the end is still to come.

The Bible gives a very honest and detailed account of how the various followers of Christ responded to the news of the empty grave. Not all were excited and not all believed. This rings true today when Christians respond to global events. Some have the mental ability to OBSERVE Christ in the CONTEXT of His sovereignty and therefore have the PERSPECTIVE that He is building His Kingdom in a glorious way. Others fail to see Christ but ascribe news to the anti-Christ, the devil or simply to the evil plans of man. The old saying is true: *Some people want things to happen. Some people make things happen. And most people wonder what in the world is happening.*

In Mark 16:9-11 we read how the apostles reacted in disbelief to the news of the empty grave: *"When they heard that Jesus was alive and that she had seen him, **they did not believe it.**"* How painfully sad, but it doesn't stop there. Even more witnesses appeared later[65] but could still not persuade the followers of Christ that He was who He said He was. The unbelief of His followers eventually evoked an uncharacteristic rebuke from the Lord, disappointed at their disbelief and stubborn refusal to listen to the words of those who saw Him[66].

Luke confirms the stories in Mark and in John but with a more telling referral. Luke mentions that the disciples did not believe the report of the women because they thought it sounded foolish. Peter, however sprinted over to the grave to see for himself, seeing the linens set aside, he went off in a quandary, pondering what had happened. Others beside the apostles had different reactions to the empty graves. Luke also states that Jesus rebuked their foolish and slow hearts for not believing (Luke 24:25-26).

Mary's perspectives however were formed by what she knew, not by what she saw. For her it was a matter of *"Know Christ, know resurrection."* Peter and John's perspectives were formed **by what they didn't see.** For them it

---

[65] Mark 16:12-13 Afterward Jesus appeared in a different form to two of them while they were walking in the country. These returned and reported it to the rest; but they did not believe them either.
[66] Mark 16:14 Later Jesus appeared to the Eleven as they were eating; he rebuked them for their lack of faith and their stubborn refusal to believe those who had seen him after he had risen.

was a matter of: *"No Christ, no resurrection."* They still did not have the ability to build their mental capacity. After three years of following the Master they still did not understand the Biblical interpretation from a redemptive perspective. It once again confirms that we *can only see what we are giving attention to.*

Expanding our mental capacity will therefore be determined by the glasses we have on. Only by looking through God's lenses will we be able to get the CHRIST perspective and not the WORLD perspective. Only by Expanding our mental capacity will we be able to seek the REDEMPTIVE and not get side-tracked by the PROPHETIC, as important as that might be.

Once you see it, you cannot *not* see it.

Amazingly, once we start building our mental capacity and look through lenses of redemption, we will soon discover the need to build our emotional capacity.

CHAPTER 6
Emotional Capacity
We need to develop our affection

One of the most convicting and uncompromising verses in the Bible is found in 1 John 4:8: *Whoever does not love does not know God, because God is love*. There must therefore be an expansion of our EMOTIONAL CAPACITY if we want to grow and mature as believers.

Love is not a mere **ATTRIBUTE** of God; like light, it is His **NATURE**. This does not mean that loving is one of God's activities, but that every activity of God is loving. If He creates, He creates in love. If He rules, He rules in love. If He judges, He judges in love. Everything He does expresses His nature. God and His nature are manifested by what He does. By love God is revealed and known, and this therefore becomes the indwelling nature of every follower of Christ. He that does not love the image of God in His people, has no saving knowledge of God. God is love and therefore His followers need to be the embodiment of His love.

To love God and to love our neighbour is the law on which all virtues hang[67], and the pursuit of a bigger capacity to love should be first and foremost on every follower's agenda. This is a non-negotiable. The ability to love deeply, unconditionally and uncompromisingly should be developed before seeking any other virtue. It is ranked by God even higher than truth.

Building our emotional capacity through the vehicle of overflowing love is the heart cry of Paul for the Church throughout the ages: "May the Lord

---

[67] Mark 12:29-31 "The most important one," answered Jesus, "is this: 'Hear, O Israel: The Lord our God, the Lord is one. Love the Lord your God with all your heart and with all your soul and with all your mind and with all your strength.' The second is this: 'Love your neighbor as yourself.' There is no commandment greater than these."

make your love increase and overflow for each other and for everyone else, just as ours does for you." (1 Thessalonians 3:12)

Please press the pause button for a moment and let this sink in:
In Colossians 3 Paul provides a comprehensive list of virtues that should be the adornments on the robe of every believer. *"Clothe yourselves,"* he says, (12) *"with compassion, kindness, humility, gentleness, patience, forbearance and forgiveness."* And once again, like in most of his letters, Paul ends with the one virtue that contains the whole of Christian perfection, and links all the parts of it together, and, surprise surprise, it is not TRUTH, it is LOVE.

When Paul refers to the word "bond" in "bond of perfectness"[68] he uses the Greek word *SUNDESMOS*, which is also the word used for LIGAMENT. Love is therefore the ligament that binds all virtues into perfection. This is extremely significant and intentional. A ligament is a short band of tough, flexible, fibrous connective tissue which connects two bones or cartilages or holds together a joint. It is also a membranous fold that supports an organ and keeps it in position.

From a spiritual perspective therefore love, or charity, is a tough but flexible virtue that links together all other virtues. It protects the body and keeps it in the right position before God, who is the Author and Perfector of love. This does not minimise the importance of truth, or any other virtue for that matter, but it does emphasise the fact that love contains the ability to join together and unite, more than any virtue.

In a sense truth **holds** all virtues together while love **links** all virtues together. The reason is simple. Truth cannot, and should not, be compromising and flexible. Truth is firm and has a firm foundation. But of equal importance is the fact that love cannot, and should not, be rigid and unbending. Paul explains in 1 Timothy 1:5 that *"the goal of our instruction is love from a pure heart and a good conscience and a sincere faith."* Note

---

[68] Colossians 3:14 And above all these things put on charity *(love)*, which is the bond of perfectness. (KJV)

that truth is not the goal, love is. Truth is the means. It is subordinate. Truth serves love. Education serves relationships — mainly the relationship between us and God, but also between Christian and Christian, and between us and unbelievers. The "goal" of truth is ultimately to reveal the true nature of God: LOVE.

This ligament of Biblical virtue needs to be flexible and compassionate. Love does not rejoice IN truth but WITH truth[69]. Love shapes how we **speak** the truth[70] while truth shapes how we **show** love[71].

But loving mostly comes naturally with those we like. Expanding a capacity to love more will involve loving the "unlovable" people who differ from us, those who irritate us and even those, or especially those, who seek to harm us. This was the message of Matthew 5 and this was the heart of Christ (verse 44) when He instructed His followers to love their enemies and pray for those who persecute them. The reason was simple; because God is a good God who gives in excess and *"causes his sun to rise on the evil and the good, and sends rain on the righteous and the unrighteous"*, His followers are expected to do the same. Mediocrity, and just doing the bare minimum and loving those who deserve our love, was never an option.

Growing our capacity to love more and to love differently will be one of the major, but at the same time most rewarding, challenges we will face on our journey with Christ. GOD IS LOVE. This is His nature and His DNA. Anybody who confesses to be in Christ has no option but to reflect this incarnated unconditional character trait. Love is the ID document of those who claim to belong to the Kingdom of God. Think about the exposition in John 4:7-21 that challenges every believer to love, not as an observation but as a demonstration: (emphasis from the author)

---

[69] 1 Corinthians 13:6 Love does not delight in evil but rejoices with the truth.

[70] *Ephesians 4:15 Instead, speaking the truth in love, we will grow to become in every respect the mature body of him who is the head, that is, Christ.*

[71] *1 John 5:2-3 This is how we know that we love the children of God: by loving God and carrying out his commands. In fact, this is love for God: to keep his commands. And his commands are not burdensome*

*1 John 4:7-21 Dear friends, let us love one another, **for love comes from God**. Everyone who loves has been born of God and knows God. Whoever does not love does not know God, **because God is love**. This is how God showed his love among us: He sent his one and only Son into the world that we might live through him. This is love: not that we loved God, but that he loved us and sent his Son as an atoning sacrifice for our sins. Dear friends**, since God so loved us, we also ought to love one another.** No one has ever seen God; but if we love one another, **God lives in us and his love is made complete in us.** This is how we know that we live in him and he in us: He has given us of his Spirit. And we have seen and testify that the Father has sent his Son to be the Savior of the world. If anyone acknowledges that Jesus is the Son of God, God lives in them and they in God. And so we know and rely on the love God has for us. **God is love. Whoever lives in love lives in God, and God in them.** This is how love is made complete among us so that we will have confidence on the day of judgment: In this world we are like Jesus. **There is no fear in love.** But perfect love drives out fear, because fear has to do with punishment. The one who fears is not made perfect in love. **We love because he first loved us.** Whoever claims to love God yet hates a brother or sister is a liar. **For whoever does not love their brother and sister, whom they have seen, cannot love God,** whom they have not seen. And he has given us this command: Anyone who loves God must also love their brother and sister.*

Love cannot be contained in the same heart that is filled with fear, suspicion and hatred. We cannot have Christ and not have unconditional love. It is as simple as that. If we struggle to love, we have not yet been transformed and need to build capacity in this regard. Don't go over this chapter too quickly and don't simply dismiss new thoughts as "not for me" teachings. Here are four kinds of love that we are seldom taught:

- A Kenosis love
- A Glasnost love
- A Sine qua non love
- An Empath's love

A KENOSIS LOVE

Kenosis, as a Christian definition, is the act of emptying oneself of one's own will and becoming entirely receptive to God's divine will. It is embodied in Christ Emmanuel by the renunciation of His divine nature and becoming incarnated into the world. In Christian theology, and what it means to every believer, **kenosis** is the principle described in Philippians 2:7 where we read that Jesus "*made himself nothing*".

Kenosis love, or self-emptying love, is also revealed magnificently in the Trinity. God the Father, who is Love, completely empties Himself into the Son; the Son empties into the Spirit; and the Spirit empties into the Father. Incarnation flows from this kenosis that is inherent to God's nature. It is a self-emptying love that exists for the benefit of others. This is, as Cynthia Breault writes, "*the way of kenosis, the revolutionary path that Jesus introduced into the consciousness of the West*."

Cynthia explains: "*For the vast majority of the world's spiritual seekers, the way to God is "up." Deeply embedded in our religious and spiritual traditions—and most likely in the human collective unconscious itself—is a kind of compass that tells us that the spiritual journey is an ascent, not a descent. And yet Jesus had only one "operational mode". . . "down" In whatever life circumstance, Jesus always responded with the same motion of self-emptying—or to put it another way, the same motion of descent: going lower, taking the lower place, not the higher.*"

Jesus' entire life demonstrates how God loves with an unconditional and selfless kenosis love. For God so loved... that He gave (John 3:16); a self-emptying love. Why hasn't Western Christianity emphasized what seems so obvious and clear? If we truly seek to build capacity and to contain more of Christ, the route is "down". Not getting fuller with love but emptier of ourselves.

This KENOSIS LOVE was always the subject of Jesus' teachings and is why He focused on self-denial and not self-enrichment:

- *Mark 9:35 Sitting down, Jesus called the Twelve and said, "Anyone who wants to be first must be the very last, and the servant of all."*
- *Mark 8:34 Then he called the crowd to him along with his disciples and said: "Whoever wants to be my disciple must deny themselves and take up their cross and follow me."*

The irony in Jesus' teaching, as Richard Rohr puts it, is that: *"when I'm nothing, I'm everything. When I'm empty, I'm full. This is why so few people truly seek an authentic spiritual life. Who wants to be nothing? We've been told the whole point was to be somebody. The ego is naturally attracted to heroic language, and so we focused on the heroic instead of transformation. Jesus' teaching was more about becoming a loving, humble, and servant-like person than a hero by any of our normal standards."*

John of the Cross expressed it this way[72]:
To come to the pleasure you have not, you must go by a way in which you enjoy not. To come to the knowledge you have not, you must go by a way in which you know not. To come to the possession you have not, you must go by a way in which you possess not. To come to be what you are not, you must go by a way in which you are not.
But Kenosis love must be revealed as Glasnost love

A GLASNOST LOVE

During the days of Glasnost (openness) and Perestroika (reformation), when the USSR started the arduous process of opening up its borders to the "outside world" and many mission organizations from the West shifted their attention to this new field of ministry, the Orthodox Church in Russia realized the dangers of foreign theologies and became suspicious of any stranger attending a service.

---

[72] John of the Cross, *The Ascent of Mount Carmel*. See *John of the Cross: Selected Writings*, ed. Kieran Kavanaugh (Paulist Press: 1987), 44-45.

One of my colleagues, visiting Leningrad (St Petersburg) during this time attended a Russian Orthodox Church on a Sunday morning with a desire to celebrate communion with local brothers and sisters. When the priest approached my friend, there was an immediate hesitation and the priest refused to offer the bread and wine to this suspicious looking stranger. Deeply saddened my friend got up and left the Church, heartbroken that after many years of service in this nation he loved so much, he was unable to celebrate the bread and wine with people he loved and respected.

After walking for a few blocks, he suddenly realized that he was being followed by the brother that sat next to him in Church. The man ran after him with his cup and piece of bread in his hand and asked if he could serve my friend and offer him communion in the street. My friend was overwhelmed by this gesture of solidarity. He looked at the man and asked the obvious question, *"Why are you doing this when your priest refused to serve me?"* The answer was clear: *"My brother, sometimes you need to love people more than your Church allows you to."*

These words, and this principle, have stuck with me for the past 30 years of ministry; to have a Glasnost love, an open love that passes all understanding, all borders and defies all reasoning. To have an openness to love more than is allowed, to risk more than is required, to encourage more than is deserved, to sacrifice more than is expected, to be kinder than is anticipated, to trust more than is reasonable, to work harder than is demanded, to give more than is necessary and an openness to bless more than is anticipated.

Capacity building will not be determined IF we love, but HOW we love. The following was found written on the wall in Mother Teresa's home for children in Calcutta:

- People are often unreasonable, irrational, and self-centred. Forgive them anyway.
- If you are kind, people may accuse you of selfish, ulterior motives. Be kind anyway.

- If you are successful, you will win some unfaithful friends and some genuine enemies. Succeed anyway.
- If you are honest and sincere people may deceive you. Be honest and sincere anyway.
- What you spend years creating, others could destroy overnight. Create anyway.
- If you find serenity and happiness, some may be jealous. Be happy anyway.
- The good you do today, will often be forgotten. Do good anyway.
- Give the best you have, and it will never be enough. Give your best anyway.
- In the final analysis, it is between you and God. It was never between you and them anyway.

Oh, may God have mercy on us when we watch the news, and like Jonah of old, determine in our own minds who could be loved, who should be loved and who is undeserving of our love. May God have mercy on us when we judge those who are racially different, culturally strange or theologically odd. May we find grace to have a "Glasnost" in our hearts with an openness to love more than our community allows us to.

A SINE QUA NON LOVE

Sine qua non implies something that is absolutely indispensable or essential, a non-negotiable and a prerequisite. In the same sense that believing in Christ is a *sine qua non* for being saved, so loving our enemy and forgiving those who mean harm to us is a *sine qua non* for every follower of Christ.

The challenge however is that many things that Christians feel are *sine qua nons* or "non-negotiables" today are at major variance with what Jesus actually taught and emphasized. How can we read the eight Beatitudes and the Sermon on the Mount, for example, and not know that Jesus clearly taught love, peace, forgiveness, reconciliation, charity, nonviolence and simplicity of life? It is impossible. But what often happens is that we read these Scriptures, that deeply contradict our attitudes and our lifestyles, with lenses that disallow them to penetrate our hearts. When God's "non-negotiables" challenge our lifestyles, we tend to create new non-negotiables and dilute the essence and prerequisites of what the Gospel is all about.

We have slowly fallen away from the core of the teaching of Jesus and created, as Richard Rohr calls it, *"a new set of non-negotiables as an evacuation plan for the next world"*. The non-negotiables based on the teachings of Jesus according to Rohr include:

- Peace-making
- Love of Enemy
- Forgiveness
- Justice and Generosity to the poor
- A community based on inclusion of all not exclusion — (this is a real challenge — think about it.)

Fr. Rohr concludes by saying that *"You could say that Jesus was crucified because of who he ate with"*.

A week after the bomb blasts at two churches in Egypt that killed nearly 50 people we had the privilege to meet Pastor Sameh, the head of one of the largest Evangelical Churches in the Middle East. His words made us realise that the essence of the Gospel that we have lost in the west was still securely practised by the persecuted Church. Pastor Sameh spoke about a new-found, non-negotiable love for their "enemies": *"First the Lord had to teach us two lessons."* He said, referring to those who seek to destroy the Church, *"The first thing the Lord did: He gave us a heart of compassion for our enemy. He melted our hearts. Secondly, He taught us how to serve our enemies, how to love them by serving them."*

These words were echoed by Pastor Ramah, a leader from Homs in Syria who endured countless attacks and who survived thousands of mortars that hit their community: *"We worked day and night amongst the refugees and continually asked the Lord what we should do. The answer was always the same: LOVE THEM."*

In order to return to the non-negotiables of Scripture we need to enlarge our emotional capacity of love, peace, reconciliation and charity. This is not a quote by the author of this book but a quote from the Author of life.

AN EMPATH'S LOVE

If 2 Corinthian 1:3-4[73] is understood correctly, Christ is described as what modern phycologists would call an EMPATH. This term describes a person with high levels of care, great compassion, a born comforter who is generally very understanding of others and their positions. It is a person who often times will ask questions rather than make snap judgments, or intuitively seems to "know" there is more to a story than meets the eye. Empaths are people who don't "read" the future, they "read" people. They are able to make special connections with the people around them and can sense when they are needed.

Being an empath is not about having the ability to feel **SYMPATHY** for people but having the ability to feel **EMPATHY** with people. Sympathy is when we feel a sense of care and concern for other people. When we sympathize with someone, it means we feel compassion for them and hope that their situation improves. Empathy is the ability to feel the needs of others as if it were us. When someone is an empath, it means they have an especially deep understanding and connection to the feelings of people around them. Empaths can feel other people's feelings almost as if they were their own.

This sounds exactly like Jesus when He stood at the grave of Lazarus and wept (John 11:35), knowing well that He would raise him from the dead. Or

---

[73] 2 Corinthians 1:3-4 Praise be to the God and Father of our Lord Jesus Christ, the Father of compassion and the God of all comfort, who comforts us in all our troubles, so that we can comfort those in any trouble with the comfort we ourselves receive from God.

in Luke 19:41 when He saw the city and He wept. We read about the compassion of Jesus the empath in Luke 7:13 when He saw the dead son of a widow and He had compassion, in Matthew 9:36 when He saw the crowds and He was moved with kindness and also in Matthew 14:14 when He saw the multitude and He was moved with empathy. His words reflect someone who deeply notices the needs in others even before He recognises His own. In Matthew 15: 32, when He saw the hungry He said to His disciples, *"I have compassion on them."* In Matthew 20:34 He saw the blind man and He had compassion, as He did with the leper in Mark 1:41 and those who were like sheep without a shepherd in Mark 6:34.

Wow, what a Saviour. Not like the one who demands submission at all times but the empath, the One who is known by one word: LOVE.

Richard Rohr refers to the beatitude in Matthew 5:4 — Blessed are those who mourn — as a reference by the Lord that *"until you have cried you don't know God."*

He explains as follows:
'The Syrian Fathers Ephrem and Simeon weren't as familiar in Western Christianity as the Greek and Latin Fathers after the early centuries of the Church. The Greek and Latin Fathers tended to filter the Gospel through the head; the Syrian Fathers' theology was much more localized in the body. They actually proposed that tears be a sacrament in the Church. Saint Ephrem went so far as to say until you have cried you don't know God.

'Tears seem ridiculous in a culture like ours which Is so focused on diversions and entertainment, and are especially a stumbling block to men. Crying will make us look vulnerable. We must teach all young people how to cry. Now, in my later years, I finally understand why Saints Francis and Clare cried so much, and why the saints spoke of "the gift of tears".'

But, ultimately, in one way or another, the character traits of an empath should be evident in the life of anyone who dares to follow Christ, the

Father of compassion. The challenge in an age of anger, suspicion and self-fulfilment is how to enlarge this capacity and develop this character trait.

So how do we enlarge our emotional capacity to love and care more?

According to *Higher Perspectives*[74] empaths are very special people and if you have one in your life you can consider yourself lucky. Here are ten ways to spot an empath but also ten guidelines to how you can develop the capacity to become one...

1. **Empaths experience the emotions of other people** almost as strongly as they experience their own emotions and feel the pain of others intensely, as described in Hebrews 13:3 *Continue to remember those in prison as if you were together with them in prison, and those who are mistreated as if you yourselves were suffering.*
2. **Empaths don't want to be a burden**, so they hide their own emotions. They have the ability to feel happy when those around them are happy and down when those around them are down. Empaths are so emotionally connected to others that they experience the emotions of others almost as if they were their own, as described in 1 Corinthians 12:26 *If one part suffers, every part suffers with it; if one part is honored, every part rejoices with it.*
3. Since **empaths are constantly in touch** with the emotions of the people they are with, they may avoid contact in order to take a break. Spending some time alone means the empath can have some time to recover from feeling emotionally drained, as described in Luke 6:12 *when Jesus went out to a mountainside to pray, and spent the night praying to God.*
4. **Empaths have a special ability to see through other people**. One of the ways this manifests itself is in an empath's ability to detect lies. An empath can easily detect lies because they are able to read a person's emotions and true intentions, as described in Matthew 26:23 when Jesus looked at Judas and said, *"The one who has dipped his hand into the bowl with me will betray me."*

---

[74] http://www.higherperspectives.com/empath-2505318837.html

5. **Empaths spend a lot of time and energy tending to other people's needs**. Empaths feel a deep need to help others, as described in Mark 6:34 *when Jesus saw a large crowd and He had compassion on them, because they were like sheep without a shepherd.*
6. **Empaths have the ability to love deeply**. As with all of the emotions they experience, an empath will feel love very deeply. This love extends from their spouse or partner to their family and to all of the people in their lives. Empaths make the people in their lives feel extremely loved and cared for, as described in Matthew 20:34, *Jesus had compassion on them and touched their eyes. Immediately they received their sight and followed him.*
7. **Empaths also have a strong appreciation for society** in general as described in Matthew15:32 when Jesus called His disciples to Him and said, *"I have compassion for these people; they have already been with me three days and have nothing to eat. I do not want to send them away hungry, or they may collapse on the way.."*
8. **Empaths will always look out for the underdog**: Anyone who is suffering, in emotional pain or being bullied draws an empath's attention and compassion, as described in Mark 6:35 *when He fed the multitudes.*
9. **Empaths always strive for the truth,** as Jesus described Himself in John 14:6 *"I am the way and the truth and the life. No one comes to the Father except through me."*
10. **Empaths are excellent listeners**. An empath won't talk about themselves much unless it's to someone they really trust. They love to learn and know about others and genuinely care as described in Matthew 20:32 when Jesus stopped on His journey and called the blind men with these words: *"What do you want me to do for you?"*

If you have an empath in your life, count yourself lucky. If you know someone who needs an empath in their life, enlarge your capacity and be one.

Amazingly, once we start building our emotional capacity we will soon discover the need to build our intentional capacity.

CHAPTER 7
Intentional Capacity
We need to choose our response

This chapter is not about having a *"purpose driven life"* but *"living an intentional life"*. The difference is subtle yet defining. **Purpose** is what we try to achieve or an aim and a goal we set ourselves. A *"purpose driven life"* relates to what we wish to accomplish and answers the *"why we do what we do"* of our spiritual journey. **Intention** sets the direction of the mind towards what we intend to do and the choices we make. *"Living an intentional life"* refers to our resolve and answers the *"why we choose what we choose"* on our spiritual journey. There must be an expansion of our INTENTIONAL CAPACITY if we want to grow and mature as believers.

Living an intentional life is reflected in the heart of Joshua when he gives the people of Israel the following option: (Joshua 24:15) *"... **choose** for yourselves this day whom you will serve, whether the gods your ancestors served beyond the Euphrates, or the gods of the Amorites, in whose land you are living. But as for me and my household, we will serve the LORD."*

Matthew Henry explores Joshua 24:15 as follows:
"Never was any treaty carried on with better management, nor brought to a better issue, than this of Joshua with the people, to engage them to serve God. Would it be any obligation upon them if they made the service of God their choice? — he here puts them to their choice because it would have a great influence upon their perseverance [capacity building] in religion if they embraced it with the reason of men and with the resolution of men.

These two things he here brings them to...
- *Firstly he brings them to embrace their religion RATIONALLY and intelligently, for it is a reasonable service. It is God's will that this service should be, not our chance, or a force upon us, but our choice.*
- *Secondly, he brings them to embrace their religion RESOLUTELY, and*

to express a full purpose of heart to cleave to the Lord."

One area of human nature that is too often neglected in teachings is the choice-making component of our spiritual journey. We are keen to emphasise the indwelling of the Spirit and that we are dead to the world, but we neglect to highlight the need to expand our intentional capacity of preferences and choices. When Jesus finds His disciples sleeping in His hour of need (Matthew 26:40) He warns them not to fall into temptation because even though *"the spirit is willing, the flesh is weak"*.

Scripture constantly warns believers to intentionally choose the way of the Lord, and to do it today:

- *Joshua 24:15 But if serving the LORD seems undesirable to you, **then choose for yourselves this day** whom you will serve, whether the gods your ancestors served beyond the Euphrates, or the gods of the Amorites, in whose land you are living. But as for me and my household, we will serve the LORD.*
- *Deuteronomy 30:19 This day I call the heavens and the earth as witnesses against you that I have set before you life and death, blessings and curses. **Now choose** life, so that you and your children may live .*
- *Psalm 119:30 **I have chosen** the way of faithfulness; I have set my heart on your laws.*
- *Psalm 119:173 May your hand be ready to help me, for **I have chosen** your precepts.*
- *Psalm 25:12 Who, then, are those who fear the LORD? He will instruct them in the ways **they should choose.***
- *Romans 2:18 You know what God wants you to do, and you have learned from the Law **to choose** what is right.*

The mind governed by the flesh is death warns Romans 8:6. *The mind governed by the flesh is hostile to God*, councils the next verse (Romans 8:7) and *those who are in the realm of the flesh cannot please God*, one verse further (Romans 8:8).

Galatians 5:17 warns us that the flesh desires what is contrary to the Spirit, and the Spirit what is contrary to the flesh. *They are in conflict with each other.*

Watchman Nee, in his book "The Spiritual Man[75]" says: "*the mind of man is his organ of thought. But not only is it equipped to know, think, imagine, remember, and understand, it also constitutes a battlefield where Satan and his evil spirits contend against the truth and hence against the believer. We may illustrate as follows. Man's will and spirit are like a citadel which the evil spirits crave to capture. The open field where the battle is waged for the seizure of the citadel is man's mind. Note how Paul the Apostle describes it: "though we live in the world we are not carrying on a worldly war, for the weapons of our warfare are not worldly but have divine power to destroy strongholds. We destroy arguments and every proud obstacle to the knowledge of God, and take every thought captive to obey Christ" (2 Cor. 10.3-5).*

Paul initially tells us of a battle—then where the battle is fought—and finally for what objective. This struggle pertains exclusively to man's mind. The Apostle likens man's arguments or reasonings to an enemy's strongholds. He pictures the mind as held by the enemy; it must therefore be broken into by waging war. He concludes that many rebellious thoughts are housed in these strongholds and need to be taken captive to the obedience of Christ. All this plainly shows us that the mind of man is the scene of battle where the evil spirits clash with God. The mind is a battle field and our choices will ultimately determine our actions. Building capacity in our intentions will involve four areas of growth:

- Intent of the soul
- Intent in Gethsemane
- Intent on a third way
- Intent as integrity

---

[75] http://www3.telus.net/trbrooks/mindbattlefield.htm

INTENT OF THE SOUL

F.M.Perry shares a teaching on the internet[76] that should be re-examined and re-assessed in our quest to expand our capacity to choose wider in order to live deeper.

Perry argues from the Scripture in 1 Thessalonians 5:23[77] that the complete makeup of a human being can be described with a combination of three different words: spirit and soul and body.

The words spirit, soul, and body are translated from the three original New Testament Greek words: *pneuma, psyche*, and *soma*, respectively. In the original Hebrew language of the Old Testament the same three words are *ruach, nephesh* and *geshem*, respectively. Considering the usage throughout the Old and New Testaments of these three different words, Perry concludes each words has a different meaning. A spirit is somewhat different from a soul or a body. And a soul is somewhat different from a body or a spirit. Paul used all three words to describe the complete or entire makeup of a person. We are led to the thought that each human being must be composed of three different entities which Paul calls: spirit and soul and body.

The body and spirit components of every human being are more easily identifiable than the soul. According to Scripture the human body was formed by God "of dust from the ground" and God gave spirit to the human being when He "breathed into his nostrils the breath of life[78]". When God formed the body of the human from dust and imparted life to him by "breathing (a spirit) into his nostrils", "man became a living soul". The body is God-formed. The spirit is God-given. With these gifts, man becomes a unique living soul.

---

[76] http://www.faithhopelove.net/SpiritandSoulandBody.html
[77] 1Thessalonians 5:23 May God himself, the God of peace, sanctify you through and through. May your whole spirit, soul and body be kept blameless at the coming of our Lord Jesus Christ.
[78] Genesis 2:7 Then the LORD God took some soil from the ground and formed a man out of it; he breathed life-giving breath into his nostrils and the man began to live.

Human beings, therefore, have both body and spirit. But the human characteristic that is more than just body and spirit is called soul. Human beings are living souls.

In Genesis 2:7 we find that "the LORD God formed a man from the dust of the ground and breathed into his nostrils the breath of life, and the man became a living being (soul)". When God formed the body of man from dust and gave a spirit to him by breathing into his nostrils, "man became a living soul". This is confirmed in 1 Corinthians 15:45 where Paul writes: "So it is written: "The first man Adam became a living being (soul)." The soul (life) is therefor the connection between body and spirit. It is, as Derek Prince rightly describes it; *"The body was clay infused by divine life. The soul came about through the union of Spirit and body."*

The soul represents the unique human personality, that which makes us who we are. The soul is the "intentional" component of our human nature, the decision-making unit, the who I am and what I feel. The soul becomes the "policymaking" unit in our bodily armour.

That is why David declares in Psalm 103 *"Bless the Lord O my soul"*. David is intentionally calling on his soul to choose to worship the Lord. In Psalm 6:3 the Psalmist confirms that his "soul is in deep anguish". In Psalm 57:8 the Psalmist calls out "Awake, my soul!" If we want to expand our capacity as believers it will involve our souls and demand that godly decisions are made in the difficult times of our lives

Perry concludes with these words: *"The complete human being is God's creation. The unique body of each human was made by God. The unique spirit of each human came from God. Then, as the spirit quickened the body, God made in the human certain characteristics which were tantamount to a third part, a unique living soul. The human was then fully created as a unique living person, a triune being, with a consciousness of himself."*

It is this consciousness that we need to develop intentionally.

INTENT IN GETHSEMANE

Jesus presented His followers with a calling that required life choices that few accepted. It was a calling that would ultimately lead to death and although thousands followed Him, only a handful imitated Him.

This still applies today. Millions follow Christ as Lord but those who choose to make Him Lord of all, are far fewer in number. The challenge for every believer is to make "life-choices" before "life happens" and not to trust ourselves to make intentional choices on the spur of the moment and hope our capacity would then increase. We have to make choices in advance in order to face our "moments of truth" without any doubt.

Dietrich Bonhoeffer, a German pastor and author of the classic book "The Cost of Discipleship", became known for his staunch resistance to the Nazi dictatorship. He was arrested in April 1943 by the Gestapo and executed by hanging in April 1945. While imprisoned at a Nazi concentration camp, Bonhoeffer wrote the following on embracing persecution:

"When Christ calls a man he bids him come and die. The Christian life is a crucified life. 'Take up your cross and follow Me...' was the command of Jesus. 'I am crucified with Christ' was the confession of Paul. But just as we must all take up our cross daily and be crucified with Christ, before we get to Calvary, we always pass through Gethsemane; the place where our will meets the will of God. It is here, in this garden, that the battle is fought – and either won or lost. The Roman soldiers did not take Jesus' life when they crucified Him. He had already laid it down Himself. You cannot kill a man who is already dead! Jesus was victorious at Calvary because He was victorious in Gethsemane. The disciples faltered and fled at the crucifixion because they slept in Gethsemane. Gethsemane is the place where you make the decision every day to get on the cross or to run from it."

The truth is that this capacity building will not come easy. Choosing to forgive those who hurt us is not the easy option but not doing it will have far more devastating effects; it will stop capacity growth. Choosing to love our enemies will never come naturally and will require intentional Gethsemane moments, relentlessly, progressively and continuously.

INTENT ON A THIRD WAY

I am always amazed at the willingness of believers to pray for change but how often we find it difficult to become the agents of the change we pray for. When calls are made for believers to pray for justice, a stop to corruption and crime-free communities thousands turn up and bow their knees in humility before the Lord. We refer to 2 Chronicles 7:14 [that] *if my people, who are called by my name, will humble themselves and pray and seek my face and turn from their wicked ways, then I will hear from heaven, and I will forgive their sin and will heal their land.*
Sadly, while bowing down and offering our prayers, we often forget that this Scripture refers to the attitude of prayer more than the action of prayer. It is not the bowing of the knees that indicates humility but the surrendering of our hearts that the Lord desires. It refers to a brokenness and not a boldness. It calls believers to embrace a life of intentional love —for their enemies; intentional forgiveness — for those who harm them; a life of intentional reconciliation — for those who offend them and a life of intentional goodness — to those who persecute them.

But we seek justice. Where there are victims there need to be scapegoats and the guilty need to be punished. After all, we serve a God of justice and righteousness, not so?

In this regard the Lord offers His followers a third way.

So often we think that the only choice we have as believers is either retaliation or passivity. In his books "Engaging the Powers" and "The Powers That Be", Walter Wink argues that Jesus rejected these two common ways of responding to injustice: violent resistance and passive acceptance. Instead, Jesus advocated a third way: retaliating with an assertive but non-violent response.

The key to understanding Wink's argument is a detailed attention to the social customs of the Jewish homeland in the first century and what Jesus' sayings would have meant in that context. To illustrate, let's look at the saying about "turning the other cheek[79]". Jesus specifies that the person has been struck on the right cheek, not just the cheek. How can you be struck on the right cheek? As Wink emphasises, you have to act this out in order to get the point: you can be struck on the right cheek only by an open hand blow with the left hand, or with a backhand blow from the right hand (try it). However, in that culture, people did not use the left hand to strike others. It was reserved for "unseemly" uses. Thus, being struck on the right cheek meant that one had been backhanded with the right hand. Given the social customs of the day, a backhand blow was the way a superior hit an inferior, whereas one fought social equals with fists.

This means the teaching of Jesus presupposes a setting in which a superior is beating an inferior, a "majority" is picking on a "minority", or simply the "advantaged" (politically or economically) are looking down on the "disadvantaged". What should the response be? "*Turn the other cheek*" are the words of Christ. (Don't stop reading here – this has got nothing to do with passive acceptance.)

What would be the effect? The only way the superior could continue the beating would be by completely repositioning himself and giving a backhand blow with his right hand to the left cheek of the other person – which is basically impossible to do – try it. The other option was to continue with an overhand blow with the fist – which would have meant treating the inferior as an equal. Perhaps the beating would not have been stopped by this. But for the superior, it would at the very least have been disconcerting: he could continue the beating only by treating the inferior as a social peer. As Wink puts it, the inferior person was in effect saying, "I am your equal. I refuse to be humiliated anymore, but I will not resort to your tactics." That is not all. The sayings about "going the second mile" and "giving your cloak

---

[79] Matthew 5:39 But I tell you, do not resist an evil person. If anyone slaps you on the right cheek, turn to them the other cheek also.

to one who sues you for your coat" make a similar point: they suggest creative non-violent ways of protesting oppression by seeing it as an opportunity.

Christians are not people who passively accept ridicule, persecution and affliction. They retaliate! But they do not retaliate with the weapons or the attitudes of the world. Followers of Christ need to be taught that it is okay to take revenge, but that they need to use the fruit of the Spirit to do so. If someone hurts them (consider the supreme example set by Christ on the cross), we take revenge by offering forgiveness. If someone threatens our safety and security, we take revenge by praying for them. Two things will happen: "In doing this, you will heap burning coals on his head, and the LORD will reward you." (Proverbs 25:22)

William Barclay says the following: *"The simple fact is that the world will never have any use for Christianity, unless it can prove that it produces the best men and women. The authentic mark of a Christian is a life lived on the standards of Jesus Christ."*

INTENT AS INTEGRITY

Capacity building cannot take place without integrity. But not only integrity as a position, but integrity as a condition.

Integrity is mostly associated with one who strives to be UPRIGHT, HONEST, PRINCIPLED or BLAMELESS. It mostly refers to how other people see us and our *position* in society.

But amazingly this is not what the word in essence means. The meaning of the English word INTEGRITY is to be found in the original Latin word INTEGER, which means: UNTOUCHED, UNDIVIDED or WHOLE. It refers mainly to how the Lord sees us and our *condition* in society.

Think about other words from the same root:
- INTEGER in Mathematics is a *WHOLE* number

- INTEGRATE in society is to bring together, unite, combine or incorporate parts into a **WHOLE**
- INTEGRAL: relating to, or belonging as a part of the **WHOLE**
- INTEGRITY: adherence to moral and ethical principles; soundness of moral character; honest commitment to principle

In essence the word means: untouched, hence undivided and whole. This brings a whole new understanding to the concept of living a life with integrity. It is not so much to be holy, but to be wholly. Even in a sense to be wholly holy.

Think about the following verses in the Bible that refer to integrity:
- *Ephesians 6:7 Serve wholeheartedly, as if you were serving the Lord, not people.*
- *Psalm 41:12 Because of my integrity you uphold me and set me in your presence forever (wholeness).*
- *Proverbs 11:3 The integrity of the upright guides them, but the unfaithful are destroyed by their duplicity (wholeness and division).*
- *2 Corinthians 1:12 Now this is our boast: Our conscience testifies that we have conducted ourselves in the world, and especially in our relations with you, with integrity and godly sincerity. We have done so, relying not on worldly wisdom but on God's grace.*
- *Titus 2:7 In everything set them an example by doing what is good. In your teaching show integrity, seriousness.*

A perfect example in this regard is a marriage. There cannot be integrity in a marriage if there is not wholeness. When Christ refers to the bride He refers to His Church, restored in full wholeness and spending eternity with the Groom.

John 3:29 The bride belongs to the bridegroom. The friend who attends the bridegroom waits and listens for him, and is full of joy when he hears the bridegroom's voice. That joy is mine, and it is now complete (whole).

When we intentionally seek to build capacity we need to pursue wholeness. For businesses, Churches, ministries and groups, the mandate is clear:
The team's integrity **depends on the team's wholeness**
The team's wholeness **depends on the individual's integrity**
The individual's integrity **depends on the individual's wholeness**

Richard Rohr:
"At the New Jerusalem Community in Cincinnati I had "70 x 7" painted over the main doorway. New mail carriers thought it was the address! It was our address, in a way. It is the distinctive hallmark of a people liberated by Christ. Community is not where forgiveness is unnecessary or unneeded. It is where forgiveness is very free to happen. And if it doesn't happen—on a daily basis—there will be no community; without forgiveness the logic of victimhood and perpetrator rules instead of the illogic of love.

"MATURE RELIGION serves as a conveyor belt for the evolution of HUMAN CONSCIOUSNESS. Let me describe God's universal love as best I can: love is recognizing oneself in the other by realizing they are not other! We are all in this together."

Unless we can truly expand our capacity to make Godly choices our bottles will remain small and unable to contain the spiritual riches of a Saviour who died and rose again. And amazingly, once we start building our intentional capacity we will soon discover the need to expand our geographical capacity.

CHAPTER 8
Geographical Capacity
We need to shift our boundaries

One of the major obstacles in modern Christianity is the notion that the command to GO[80] is an option. This is not something we will openly confess but a thought we entertain when Scriptures confront our comfort zones. Once we choose to expand our intentional capacity, there must be an expansion of our **GEOGRAPHICAL CAPACITY** if we want to grow and mature as believers.

Before understanding the necessity of expanding our geographical capacity we need to understand exactly what it means to "enlarge our territory" or to "step out of our comfort zones" as it is so often referred to. Why is it wrong to have a comfort zone and is it even necessary to attempt "boundary shifting" when all is going well "on the inside"?

Well, to start with, the reality of human nature is that faith, and growth for that matter, only start once we exit our comfort zones. As human beings we prefer to move within an artificial mental boundary that provides the security and safety and the feelings and sense of — well — comfort. Within this artificial comfort zone, everything is routine, familiar and safe. There is no need for a deep intimate trust in a God who provides and protects and there is certainly no need for a faith that dwells in the unseen and uncertainties of life. This is one of the reasons why the abundance of Europe has led to a secularism that has robbed people of faith for decades now. The safety and security provided within the borders of human rights,

---

[80] Matthew 28:19 Therefore go and make disciples of all nations, baptizing them in the name of the Father and of the Son and of the Holy Spirit,
Acts 1:8 But you will receive power when the Holy Spirit comes on you; and you will be my witnesses in Jerusalem, and in all Judea and Samaria, and to the ends of the earth."

freedom of choice and democracy has sadly not resulted in the expansion of the Kingdom of God, as one would expect, but rather kept most people imprisoned in their own comfort zones created through independent self-sufficiency. After all, why break a routine if it's comfortable?

Ran Zilca, in an article in *Psychology Today*, explains it as follows:
"We live in a society where comfort has become a value and a life goal. But comfort reduces our motivation for introducing important transformations in our lives. Sadly, being comfortable often prohibits us from chasing our dreams. Many of us are like lions in the zoo: well-fed but sit around passively stuck in a reactive rut. Comfort equals boring shortsightedness, and a belief that things cannot change. Your comfort zone is your home base, a safe place not to stay in, but to return to, after each exhausting and exhilarating expedition through the wilderness of life. Take a look at your life today, if you are enjoying a shelter of comfort, break through it and go outside where life awaits."

The question we need to ask in essence is that if Christ was in our shoes, where would He put, or not put, the boundaries? This is the benchmark. If we can define that, then all we have to do is put our new set of boundaries around that. The question is not what we need to risk, give away or sacrifice to set a new set of boundaries outside our comfort zones but what Jesus risked, gave away and sacrificed.

In Mark 14:35-36[81] we find the ultimate example of stepping out into the unknown and forsaking security in the quest for obedience. Boundaries are shattered when Jesus utters these words, *"Yet not what I will, but what you will."*
Jesus nullifies any of His followers' pursuit of being a healthy, wealthy and prosperous Christian following a secure, safe and comfortable religion. But the act of shifting boundaries does not end as a theology in Gethsemane

---

[81] Mark 14:35-36 Going a little farther, he fell to the ground and prayed that if possible the hour might pass from him. "Abba, Father," he said, "everything is possible for you. Take this cup from me. Yet not what I will, but what you will."

and is not limited to Jesus. In John 20:19[82] Jesus appears to His disciples for the first time after His crucifixion and now passes the baton to those entrusted with the message of the Kingdom. The disciples met in secret, and hid in the safe gathering behind locked doors and the comfortable fellowship of friends and family when suddenly the Lord appears with these words: *"Peace be with you, as the Father has sent me, I am sending you[83]."*

Golgotha now moves from a full-stop, where the disciples thought it ended, to a comma, where their ministries begin. This now becomes a door to every follower of Christ to move outside the locked doors of safety and security and shift the boundaries of comfort to the ends of the earth[84]. This is a call to move as sheep among the wolves[85] and to expect discomfort and utter dependency[86]. This is the ultimate goal in setting new boundaries.

But the challenge is always in the balance. Equally important is the fact that even though this might be our ultimate goal it should not be our immediate goal in stepping out. This can only lead to discouragement and disillusionment. We need to determine the destination before we plan the route. It is a process and not an event, a marathon and not a sprint.
There are three spaces that we need in our lives if we are to build our geographical capacity:

- We need a home base
- We need a space of optimal anxiety
- We need a growth zone

---

[82] John 20:19 On the evening of that first day of the week, when the disciples were together, with the doors locked for fear of the Jewish leaders, Jesus came and stood among them and said, "Peace be with you!"
[83] John 20:21 Again Jesus said, "Peace be with you! As the Father has sent me, I am sending you."
[84] Acts 1:8 "But you will receive power when the Holy Spirit comes on you; and you will be my witnesses in Jerusalem, and in all Judea and Samaria, and to the ends of the earth."
[85] Luke 10:3 "Go! I am sending you out like lambs among wolves."
[86] John 15:20 "Remember what I told you: 'A servant is not greater than his master.' If they persecuted me, they will persecute you also. If they obeyed my teaching, they will obey yours also."

SPACE 1 — HOME BASE

Our comfort zone isn't a bad thing; far from it. We all need a space where we can relax, feel at ease and comfortable. Ran Zilca refers to a safe place, not to stay in, but to return to, after each exhausting and exhilarating expedition through the wilderness of life.

Even Jesus, who exemplifies the principle of breaking down every wall of comfort and security, had a "home base" to return to. In Matthew 4:12 we read that when Jesus heard that John had been put in prison, He withdrew to Galilee. Leaving Nazareth, He went and lived in Capernaum, which was by the lake in the area of Zebulun and Naphtali[87].

Capernaum was the home of the apostle Peter; it was also "the home base" for our Lord Jesus' earthly ministry. Here Jesus based Himself, not constantly, for He went about doing good; but this was for some time His headquarters: what little rest He had, was here; here He had a place, though not a place of His own, to lay His head on.

Capernaum was an ancient fishing village on the north shore of the Sea of Galilee in north-eastern Israel. Capernaum is mentioned 16 times in the Gospels and was the site of much of our Lord's teaching and many of His miracles and wonders. Matthew calls Capernaum Jesus' "own city", with the intent that our Lord considered it His main place of residence.

In order to build capacity we need to secure a "home base", not as a permanent fixture but as a half-way house.

---

[87] Matthew 4:13 Leaving Nazareth, he went and lived in Capernaum, which was by the lake in the area of Zebulun and Naphtali

SPACE 2 — OPTIMAL ANXIETY

Ashley Read, writer @Buffer and quoted in Frontcourt[88], refers to the place just outside of our comfort zone as a place of "optimal anxiety". It's a sweet spot of human performance and place where we're motivated to succeed. Similar to an athlete who has just prepared and warmed up for a big game, optimal anxiety is the space where we are ready to perform at our best.

The theory that anxiety can aid performance is not something new; the idea goes back to at least 1908 when Robert Yerkes and John Dodson released a study showing that arousal (anxiety) increased performance. The study also shows that only certain levels of arousal are good for performance; too much has the opposite effect and is detrimental to performance. Therefore, pushing ourselves too hard, too often and too soon can also create a notion that challenging ourselves is a negative thing and reinforce our desire to stay within our comfort zone.

But it has to be a process. I am sometimes amazed at young believers who simply want to change the world and are willing to go anywhere, and give up everything for the sake of the Kingdom. This sounds super spiritual and very convicting but the Bible gives different guidelines. First count the cost, are the words in Luke 14:28-29. If you don't, and you are unable to finish what you started, you will be ridiculed.[89]

This was more than just good advice from Christ. This was encouraging His followers to enter ministry wisely and intelligently. In the world today up to one out of two new missionaries do not last beyond their first term on the mission field[90]. In the Middle East the statistics are even worse. Nine out of every ten missionaries leave the mission field before the end of their

---

[88] https://frontcourt.media/why-leaving-your-comfort-zone-can-be-so-rewarding-backed-by-science-6b752d049a6e

[89] Luke 14:28-30 "Suppose one of you wants to build a tower. Won't you first sit down and estimate the cost to see if you have enough money to complete it? For if you lay the foundation and are not able to finish it, everyone who sees it will ridicule you, saying, 'This person began to build and wasn't able to finish.'

[90] Yohannan, K.P. 2004. Come Let's Reach the World. Carrollton, TX: GFA Books.

term due to opposition, pressures and persecution. The space of optimal anxiety needs to be carefully calculated.

This is indeed a process that needs to be repetitive and progressive: We find our home base first, then we determine the space that will provide optimal anxiety. Soon, as the borders of comfort are expanded our optimal anxiety space will grow as well and our capacity enlarges. As our newfound space, that initially presented itself as a space of "optimal anxiety", turns into a new "home base" the process needs to be repeated again and capacity will continue to grow progressively.

Equally important is finding our own personal space of "optimal anxiety". We will determine this space, no one else, and once we have moved outside our comfort zones into our "optimal anxiety zone" we can then start exploring new territories. We need to challenge ourselves in a space where we feel motivated, not where others think we need to be.

SPACE 3 — GROWTH ZONE

As we push ourselves out of our comfort zones and into a place of optimal anxiety we eventually enter our "growth zone" where challenges will become easier and our capacity expands. Eventually, things that previously scared us will become part of our new comfort zones, pushing our borders wider, thus helping us achieve more than we previously thought possible.

I remember vividly the first time we smuggled Bibles into the former USSR at the height of communism and persecution. I could hardly breathe for weeks before we travelled, I was so scared. My capacity was stretched to the limit with one single border crossing and my comfort zone changed into a new growth zone. I would never be satisfied again with the "normal" of my previous life.

The next trip to China was equally stretching but now I had a point of reference that didn't make it less daunting but at least less unfamiliar. The Lord did it once before and I knew He could do it again.

The trips that followed to Iran and Vietnam served as continued growth manoeuvres. It never became any easier than the first trip, or less unnerving, but it seemed to become a way of life and soon my new comfort zone became a ministry of taking literature into restricted areas. My capacity grew into new dimensions and new realities.

But the process made me realise that we should change the way we approach the borders of our comfort zones. Most of us view our comfort zone as a circle, with our optimal capacity outside the circle and us facing the challenge to "cross the line" into our growth zone. This can be quite intimidating.

We should rather view our comfort zone as a spiral and our optimal anxiety zone in front of us, not on the other side of the circle. The challenge of moving "outside" our comfort zones becomes less daunting when we consider we just have to move forward, in baby steps, within our current comfort zones. As we move forward our spiral automatically enlarges and we soon find ourselves on the other side of a zone that initially looked like an impenetrable border.

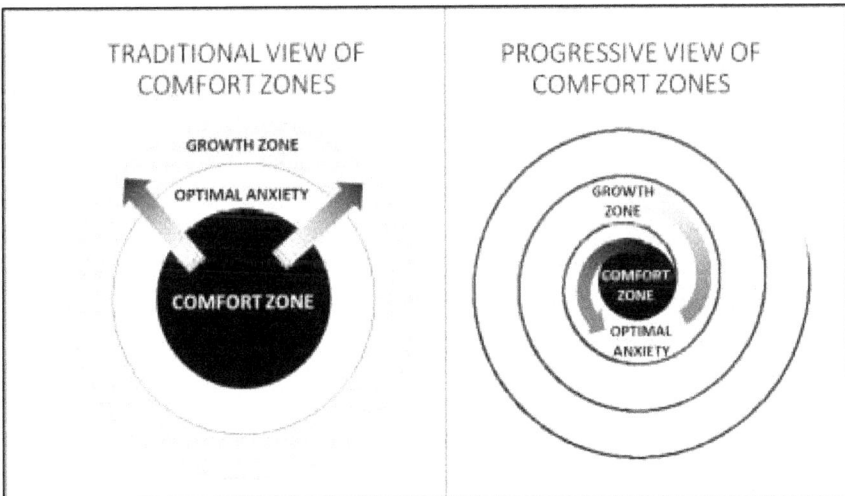

Alas, this is all theoretical and means very little if we do not move. The point of this graph is simply to illustrate that even though we only need to take small steps, they have to be intentional steps that challenge us as part of a process into the unknown.

We know a young lady, Ilana, who has had a heart for China since childhood. But, finishing school, she didn't try to break the "walls" of her comfort zone by selling everything and moving to China. She started with an achievable goal and got the spiral moving by learning Mandarin. She kept on moving forward by visiting the local Chinese Malls over weekends to practise her language skills and to befriend people. Slowly but surely the spiral started increasing and she travelled to China on a short-term outreach to envision a future there. She came back and started her fundraising endeavours with her newly-wedded husband. With the writing of the book they are on their way to China for full-time ministry. She is now on the other side of the "wall" even though she never had to break through the "wall". The spiral keeps on growing.

Another colleague of mine, Cherolyn, pursued the same process for Pakistan. She had always had a heart for missions and then equipped herself to be a teacher. She started teaching at a school near to where she grew up and became a youth worker at a local Church. After a few years she joined INcontext International and then travelled on a number of short-term outreaches to the Middle East and Asia. She was introduced to the director of a ministry in Pakistan and she has since travelled to Pakistan twice for short periods to teach at a school. She applied to join a ministry that serves in Pakistan and she is now on her way to full-time ministry. The process is never-ending but it is nevertheless one that has to start in the centre of the spiral, within our comfort zones, and as we move, the spiral grows.

How about you? Start by making friends with someone in your community; the Pakistani, Nigerian or Chinese shop-owner around the corner. Start building a friendship and then invite them for a meal. Next, visit them at their homes and get to know more about their culture. Then try to celebrate one of their feasts with them and invite them to one of your

Christian feasts, like Easter or Christmas. Start learning easy words in their language. Before you know it, the spiral is at such a point where you are ready to travel. But for God's sake, and I really mean for God's sake, enlarge your geographical capacity.

FOOTPRINTS AND FINGERPRINTS

The beauty of expanding our geographical borders is found in the opportunities to add fingerprints outside the borders of what is familiar to us, to the footprints inside the boundaries where we work, live and play.

Dr Edmond Locard, a pioneer in forensic science, was one of the founders of the International Academy of Criminalistics. Locard published over 40 books and articles in French, English, German and Spanish and conceived what is now known as Locard's Exchange.   His career was basically summarised in these words*: "Every contact leaves a trace."*

Forensic scientist Paul L Kirk explained this principle as follows:
"Wherever the criminal steps, whatever he touches, whatever he leaves, even unconsciously, will serve as a silent witness against him. Not only his fingerprints or his footprints, but his hair, the fibres from his clothes, the glass he breaks, the tool mark he leaves, the paint he scratches, the blood he deposits or collects. All of these and more, bear mute witness against him. This is evidence that does not forget. It is not absent because human witnesses are."

This is the call to us as followers of Christ: that our capacity to influence societies will translate beyond our borders of existence. There is only one question we need to ask ourselves in this regard: what footsteps do I leave behind in my community and what fingerprints do I leave behind outside my community — there where nobody has seen me or knows about me but where I have influenced the life of one other person?

What traces will we leave behind?
- When we walk in the street
- When we meet with opposition

- When we interact with one another
- When we interact with street vendors

There are many ways to expand our geographical capacity, but it will ultimately involve getting off our backsides and moving into the unknown and the unfamiliar. In this regard there really is only one certain way to succeed: TRAVEL.

Here are 25 quotes from *Expert Vagabond*[91]to whet our appetites:
1. For my part, I travel not to go anywhere, but to go. I travel for travel's sake. The great affair is to move. – Robert Louis Stevenson
2. We travel, some of us forever, to seek other places, other lives, other souls. – Anais Nin
3. I am not the same, having seen the moon shine on the other side of the world. – Mary Anne Radmacher
4. Travel makes one modest. You see what a tiny place you occupy in the world. – Gustave Flaubert
5. We travel not to escape life, but for life not to escape us. – Anonymous
6. The life you have led doesn't need to be the only life you have. – Anna Quindlen
7. Broad, wholesome, charitable views of men and things cannot be acquired by vegetating in one little corner of the earth all of one's lifetime. – Mark Twain
8. Man cannot discover new oceans unless he has the courage to lose sight of the shore. – Andre Gide
9. The world is a book, and those who do not travel read only one page. – Saint Augustine
10. Travel and change of place impart new vigour to the mind. – Seneca
11. Twenty years from now you will be more disappointed by the things you didn't do than by the ones you did do. – Mark Twain
12. Once a year, go someplace you've never been before. – Anonymous
13. Travel is the only thing you buy that makes you richer. – Anonymous

---

[91] https://expertvagabond.com/best-travel-quotes/

14. If you reject the food, ignore the customs, fear the religion and avoid the people, you might better stay at home. – James Michener
15. People don't take trips, trips take people. – John Steinbeck
16. Life is either a daring adventure or nothing. – Helen Keller
17. Stop worrying about the potholes in the road and enjoy the journey. – Babs Hoffman
18. Every man can transform the world from one of monotony and drabness to one of excitement and adventure. – Irving Wallace
19. The more I travelled the more I realized that fear makes strangers of people who should be friends. – Shirley MacLaine
20. A mind that is stretched by a new experience can never go back to its old dimensions. – Oliver Wendell Holmes
21. Life begins at the end of your comfort zone. – Neale Donald Walsch
22. One's destination is never a place, but a new way of seeing things. – Henry Miller
23. I haven't been everywhere, but it's on my list. – Susan Sontag
24. There is no moment of delight in any pilgrimage like the beginning of it. – Charles Dudley Warner
25. Investment in travel is an investment in yourself. – Matthew Karsten

Amazingly, once we start building our geographical capacity we will soon discover the need to build our risk capacity.

CHAPTER 9
Risk Capacity
We need to confront our fears

We now enter the stage where the proverbial pawpaw hits the fan. We can talk much about capacity building but unless we conquer our fears it will remain a theory. There must be an expansion of our **RISK CAPACITY** if we want to grow and mature as believers.

We are all born with natural physical and emotional needs and the inborn resources to help us fulfil them — known as human "givens". These needs must be met in order to facilitate good spiritual health. According to the Human Givens Institute[92] there are ten main innate emotional needs, and most of them are based on fears, more than needs:

1. **Security** — safe territory and an environment which allows us to develop fully
2. **Attention** (to give and receive it) — a form of nutrition
3. **Sense of autonomy and control** — having volition to make responsible choices
4. **Being emotionally connected to others**
5. Feeling **part of a wider community**
6. **Friendship, intimacy** — to know that at least one other person accepts us totally for who we are, "warts 'n' all"
7. **Privacy** — opportunity to reflect and consolidate experience
8. Sense of **status** within social groupings
9. Sense of **competence and achievement**
10. **Having meaning and purpose** — which comes from being stretched in what we do and think

---

[92] https://www.hgi.org.uk/human-givens/introduction/what-are-human-givens

WONDERFULLY FEARFUL

One of the most remarkable true stories that probably encapsulates this principle best is the story of 33-year-old Larry Walters[93].

Larry's boyhood dream was to fly. When he graduated from high school, he joined the Air Force hoping to become a pilot. Unfortunately, poor eyesight disqualified him. When he was finally discharged, he became a truck-driver and had to satisfy himself with watching jets fly over his backyard.

On July 2, 1982, Larry decided to make his dream come true. He decided to fly. He went to the local Army-Navy surplus store and purchased 45 weather balloons and several tanks of helium. The weather balloons, when fully inflated, would measure more than four feet across. Back home, Larry securely strapped the balloons to his sturdy lawn chair. He anchored the chair to the bumper of his jeep and inflated the balloons with the helium. He climbed on for a test while it was still only a few feet above the ground. Satisfied it would work, Larry packed several sandwiches and a six-pack of Miller Lite, loaded his pellet gun — figuring he could pop a few balloons when it was time to descend — and went back to the floating lawn chair. He tied himself in along with his pellet gun and provisions. Larry's plan was to lazily float up to a height of about 30 feet above his back yard after severing the anchor and in a few hours come back down.

Things didn't quite work out that way. When he cut the cord anchoring the lawn chair to his jeep, he didn't float lazily up to 30 or so feet. Instead he streaked into the LA sky as if shot from a cannon. He didn't level off at 30 feet, nor did he level off at 100 feet. After climbing and climbing, he leveled off at 11,000 feet.

At that height he couldn't risk shooting any of the balloons, lest he unbalance the load and really find himself in trouble. So he stayed there, drifting, cold and frightened, for more than 14 hours. Then he really got in

---

[93] https://www.snopes.com/travel/airline/walters.asp

trouble. He found himself drifting into the primary approach corridor of Los Angeles International Airport.

A United pilot first spotted Larry. He radioed the tower and described passing a guy in a lawn chair with a gun. Radar confirmed the existence of an object floating 11,000 feet above the airport. LAX emergency procedures swung into full alert and a helicopter was dispatched to investigate.

LAX is right on the ocean. Night was falling and the offshore breeze began to flow. It carried Larry out to sea with the helicopter in hot pursuit. Several miles out, the helicopter caught up with Larry. Once the crew determined that Larry was not dangerous, they attempted to close in for a rescue but the draft from the blades would push Larry away whenever they neared. Finally, the helicopter ascended to a position several hundred feet above Larry and lowered a rescue line. Larry snagged the line and was hauled back to shore. The difficult manoeuvre was flawlessly executed by the helicopter crew.

As soon as Larry was hauled to earth, he was immediately arrested by waiting members of the Long Beach Police Department. He was initially fined $4,000 for violations under US Federal Aviation Regulations, including operating an aircraft within an airport traffic area "without establishing and maintaining two-way communications with the control tower." Walters appealed, and the fine was reduced to $1,500. A charge of operating a "civil aircraft for which there is not currently in effect an airworthiness certificate" was dropped, as it was not applicable to his class of aircraft.

Just after landing, Walters was asked by a local reporter if he was afraid. His reply: *"Yes... wonderfully so."*

If we too can experience what it means to be "wonderfully fearful" we would be able to erase the boundaries between us and our dreams. It is a glorious victory if we can subjugate our fears to our dreams. But when the opposite happens, and fears turn into phobias and apprehension into anxiety we surrender control to an external factor that will ultimately limit our capacity and influence.

Anxiety and fear will ultimately lead to disobedience, and the more common the object of one's fear, the more limited our capacity becomes to take risks. Considering that specific phobias, or phobias tied to distinct or unique kinds of experiences, affect an estimated 19.2 million adult Americans[94] (nearly 1 in ever 200), it might be better understood why the condition should be addressed within a spiritual context as well.

Like most issues in life we must learn to control our fears and not let our fears control us. We need to determine when it is a healthy fear and when it is an unhealthy fear. To be cautious is not a bad thing but to be ruled by fear is. God gave us an "alert-system" for a good reason. When we control our anxieties, they can be put to good use. Like the fear of jumping off a cliff or the fear of breaking the law. But when our fears control us we run the risk of becoming paralysed and passive. We need to actively expand our risk capacity so that we can confront those fears that stop us from following Christ wholeheartedly. We need to discern between the good, the bad and the ugly faces of fears that seek to rule our lives.

The Lord knows our emotional needs not only from a divine perspective but especially from an emotional perspective. He walked on earth like we do. He faced the cruellest moments and felt the deepest anguish and fears. That's why we find one command in Scripture given by God to man that appears more frequently than any other.

"DO NOT BE AFRAID" — "FEAR NOT"

Depending on which translation of the Bible you use and what phrase you are searching for, the phrase *"do not fear"* or *"do not be afraid"* appears at least 130 times in the Bible (not 365 as many preachers love to proclaim). The call to "be not afraid" appears more times than the call to be holy, or

---

[94] www.womenshealth.gov/mental-health/illnesses/specific-phobias.html

the command to be obedient. This is the one character trait that God wants to instil in His followers more than anything else. The reason is obvious: Because God knows that fear paralyzes, because God knows that fear causes disobedience and because God knows that the one obstacle preventing capacity growth and holiness, is fear –not a lack of resources but FEAR, not a lack of knowledge but FEAR.

On Palm Sunday 2017 two bombs exploded in Tanta and Alexandria in Egypt. Nearly 50 people were killed and hundreds injured. ISIS officially declared war on the Church in Egypt and promised more attacks in number and more attacks in severity. When I heard the news I realised that this was a tipping point in this strategic nation. I understood that the bomb explosions could result in two responses, and two responses only. Either FEAR or FORGIVENESS. It could destroy the structures of courage that have marked the Church in Egypt for so many years or it could destroy barriers of fear and result in boldness, courage and forgiveness.

The next Sunday, on Easter Sunday, Churches were overflowing. We were in Egypt during this time and had the opportunity to meet one of the leaders of the biggest evangelical Churches in the Middle East. He shared the following: *"The two bomb blasts were answers to our prayers. We've been seeking the Lord for 30 years but the watch was not moving. We were waiting for a time such as this. This is a glorious time. It is a time for shaking, an awakening. The Spirit of fear has left us and people are running to the Lord."* He concluded with the following words: *"It is a wonderful thing when you find a key that unlocks a locked door. Forgiveness is that key."*

For believers, fear is a matter of life and death. In Genesis 3 we read how Adam and Eve took some of the forbidden fruit, ate it, immediately discovered their nakedness and hid from God. In verse 9, the Lord approaches them with this question: *"Where are you?"* God knew exactly where they were and did not ask about their **position** but about their **condition**. And then Adam answers with these words, revealing his heart in full: *"I heard you in the garden, **and I was afraid** because I was naked; so I hid."*

Fear was the first consequence of sin. This was the first emotion displayed by Adam after his first encounter with disobedience. *"I was afraid."* This was probably also the greatest achievement of Satan throughout the ages: Not getting Adam and Eve to eat from the forbidden fruit but creating fear in the hearts of the followers of God. Subsequently we find the most frequent command in Scripture by the Lord is not not to sin, BUT not to be afraid

I have travelled all over the world and have found that the one emotion that links most people together is FEAR. I have met some of the most beautiful believers who literally transform when confronted with fear. Loving people suddenly lose compassion in their fear of refugees; missional Christians fail to love Muslims; faithful followers becoming irrelevant when facing the fear of rejection. The reality is that only those who conquer fear from the inside will become relevant on the outside.

There are three reasons for fear:
- Fear has to do with PRIORITIES
- Fear has to do with PERSPECTIVES
- Fear has to do with POSITIONING

Fear has to do with PRIORITIES

What you value most will most likely determine what you fear most. If possessions are your priority then losing them will be your greatest fear and the more you have, the more you have to lose, the higher the walls and the greater the anxiety. The Lord understood this. In Luke 12:4 He clearly instructed His followers to *"be not afraid of them that kill the body, and after that have no more that they can do"*.

Obedience is simply prioritising your fears. If you fear disobedience more than death then you will be able to proclaim like Paul, (Philippians 3:7-8) *But whatever were gains to me I now consider loss for the sake of Christ. What is more, I consider everything a loss because of the surpassing worth of knowing Christ Jesus my Lord, for whose sake I have lost all things. I consider them garbage, that I may gain Christ.* The ultimate challenge for any believer is to prioritise our fears.

Jon Bloom, Staff writer, *desiringGod.org* puts it as follows:
"We tend to have too little fear for the things most dangerous to our souls, and too much fear over things far less dangerous. The fundamental question for each of us is not, "God, will you protect me from my worst fears?" but rather Jesus's question to us, "Why are you afraid?" (Matthew 8:26).

"This is the question Jesus asked his disciples in the boat when they were panicking in the storm. It was no mystery why they were afraid. A number of them were experienced boatmen who knew full well this storm could send them to their graves. They were deathly afraid of death. Jesus asked the question to get the disciples to examine where their faith was placed. To drive this home, Luke's account has Jesus asking them, "Where is your faith?" (Luke 8:25).

"Jesus asks all of us this question because he designed fear to be a faith-revealer. Fear is a gauge that tells us what we treasure (what we fear to lose and why), as well as what we believe is dangerous. Fears teach us about our own worldview."

Fear reveals our loyalties and only takes root when we have wrong priorities.

Fear has to do with PERSPECTIVES

Our perspectives always determine our actions. In the geo-political world there are seemingly more good reasons to be afraid today than in any time in history. Every day the media bombards us with news and threats of wars, disasters, plagues, economic collapses, ISIS, terrorist plots, unrest, crime, corruption and injustice. Even in the world of entertainment most movies are based on wars, horror, violence and many a genre will leave the viewer with a sense of fear or uncertainty at the least. In short, we are living within a "generation of fear".

But fears and phobias have everything to do with contextualised perspectives. Headway toward understanding symptoms of phobias was recently made with the publication of an article in *Biological Psychology*. Researchers examining fears of spiders (arachnophobia) showed that study participants who self-identified as being frightened of the creatures consistently overestimated the arachnids' size when shown contextualized photographs of this arthropod group, while at the same time failing to do so with other images, including those of butterflies.

According to neurologist and research leader Tali Leibovich, the study findings indicate *"how perception of even a basic feature such as size is influenced by emotion, and demonstrates how each of us experiences the world in a unique and different way"*. This, she added, makes room for questions as to whether an inability to correctly perceive the object of one's fear causes a phobic response, or the other way around.

This, from a spiritual perspective, becomes paramount to the healing process and building capacity. Once we look at events through "Kingdom glasses", our fears will be aligned with a sovereign God and, just like with David, giants will become slingshot targets. A fear should never be placed in an emotional perspective but rather placed next to an omnipresent, almighty God. Every fear should be seen in the context that God sovereignly appoints leaders, determines seasons and shapes history. His sovereignty becomes our fear-remover. FEAR is indeed "**False Enemy Appearing Real**". There is no neutral ground here; faith and fear cannot function from within the same soul and cannot live in the same heart. Fear only takes root when we have a wrong perspective.

Fear has to do with POSITIONING

Br Andrew once shared how he visited Corrie ten Boom just before she died. From her bed she joyfully looked at him and said the following: *"Don't look* *so sad Andrew. You have to remember to look **DOWN**."* Andrew smiled at the comment and said to Corrie *"I suppose that was a slip of the tongue, you probably mean I need to look **UP**."* "No," replied Corrie, *"you need to look down and position yourself from God's perspective and not from man's perspective."*

In Judges 7 we read the amazing account of how Gideon defeated the mighty Midianite army of 135,000 men with an army of 300 men. Gideon had enough reason to be paralysed with fear. During that night (verse 9) the LORD said to Gideon, *"Get up, go down against the camp, because I am going to give it into your hands. If you are afraid to attack, go down to the camp with your servant Purah and listen to what they are saying. Afterward, you will be encouraged to attack the camp."* So he and Purah his servant went down to the outposts of the camp and (15) when Gideon heard the dream and its interpretation, he bowed down and worshiped. He returned to the camp of Israel and called out, *"Get up! The LORD has given the Midianite camp into your hands."*

Once Gideon positioned himself to see the enemy from God's perspective, he transformed from Coward Gideon to Courageous Gideon.

Fear only takes root when we are wrongly positioned. Doug Firebaugh said *"Usually a person has more faith in their fear than faith in their future."*

Once our intentional capacity to make courageous decisions has been stretched we are able to make risky choices. We can either accommodate our fears or we can confront them. Fear can be a very powerful feeling, focused on disastrous expectations, but it is still just a feeling. It can't hurt us unless we allow it to do so. The key to the snare of fear is how we deal with it.

Defeating this paralysing emotion does not happen through positive thinking or simply by saying, "I am not going to be afraid anymore."

Paralysis is the loss of muscle function in parts of the body. It happens when something goes wrong with the way messages pass between our brain and our muscles. If we are paralysed by fear and therefore are avoiding doing something we desperately want to do, we need to take action! We need to:

- CONVERSE,
- CONFRONT AND
- CONTINUE.

Firstly, we need to CONVERSE

We need to talk to God. Fear can only be seen for what it is in the presence of the Lord. The psalmist declares in Psalm 34:4, how he *"sought the LORD, and he answered me; he delivered me from all my fears"*.

God is not a spectator in our lives. He is divinely present and firmly in control, even when things go horribly wrong. We need to take heart in how the Lord reminded His people time and time again not to be afraid

- **to Abraham in Genesis 15:1** *After this, the word of the LORD came to Abram in a vision: "Do not be afraid, Abram. I am your shield, your very great reward."*
- **to Gideon in Judges 6:23** *But the LORD said to him, "Peace! Do not be afraid. You are not going to die."*
- **to Paul in Acts 27:24** *He said, "Do not be afraid, Paul. You must stand trial before Caesar; and God has graciously given you the lives of all who sail with you."*
- **to John on the island of Patmos in Revelation 1:17** *When I saw him, I fell at his feet as though dead. Then he placed his right hand on me and said: "Do not be afraid. I am the First and the Last."*

- He spoke these words to …
- **Men like Isaac in Genesis 26:24** *That night the LORD appeared to him and said, "I am the God of your father Abraham. Do not be afraid, for I*

am with you; I will bless you and will increase the number of your descendants for the sake of my servant Abraham."

- **Women like Hagar in Genesis 21:17** *God heard the boy crying, and the angel of God called to Hagar from heaven and said to her, "What is the matter, Hagar? Do not be afraid; God has heard the boy crying as he lies there."*
- **Women like Mary in Luke 1:30** *But the angel said to her, "Do not be afraid, Mary; you have found favor with God."*
- **He spoke to individuals like Simon in Luke 5:10** *Then Jesus said to Simon, "Don't be afraid; from now on you will fish for people."*
- **and to groups and communities like the shepherds in the field in Luke 2:10** *but the angel said to them, "Do not be afraid. I bring you good news that will cause great joy for all the people."*
- **and the thousands that followed Him in Luke 12:4.** *"I tell you, my friends, do not be afraid of those who kill the body and after that can do no more."*

Jesus spoke these words with understanding and compassion to those who followed Him: *"I tell you, my friends, do not be afraid of those who kill the body and after that can do no more... Indeed, the very hairs of your head are all numbered. Don't be afraid; you are worth more than many sparrows."*

If you are overwhelmed by fear, talk to God.

Secondly, we need to CONFRONT

We need to confront the cause of the fear. Most of us find it a lot easier to accommodate our fears. We feed them and we surround ourselves with people who can feed them. We need to stop surrounding ourselves with negative people and start by confronting the things that limit capacity growth.

But it is important to realise that we do not need to confront our fears in our own strength and courage – we can stand next to the ultimate Source of strength and courage while facing our giants. This is the message the Lord gave to His followers in Matthew 28 (verses 10, 18 and 20): *"Then Jesus said to them, 'Do not be afraid... All authority in heaven and on earth has been given to Me... And surely I am with you always, to the very end of the age.'"*

Remember, rehearse and repeat the words of 1 John 4:4 *You, dear children, are from God and have overcome them, because the one who is in you is greater than the one who is in the world.*

Thirdly, we need to CONTINUE

Nowhere in Scripture does the Lord create a false sense of security in the hearts of believers and nowhere does He seek to create any illusions about the realities of life. *"You **WILL** be persecuted"* are His words to His followers. *"People **WILL** hate you for my name's sake."* The Bible is not saying: *"There is nothing scary so you don't need to be scared."* Let's be real... life is scary. That, however, does NOT mean we need to be scared of it.

BUT, the command *"do not be afraid"* more often than not is followed by an action that God is or will be taking. Here are a few such examples:

- *"Do not be afraid. Stand firm and you will see the deliverance the Lord will bring you today."* (Exodus 14:13)
- *"Do not be afraid of them; the Lord your God himself will fight for you."* (Deuteronomy 3:22)
- *"Do not be afraid of them; I have given them into your hand. Not one of them will be able to withstand you."* (Joshua 10:8)
- *"Do not be afraid, little flock, for your Father has been pleased to give you the kingdom."* (Luke 12:32)

Fear is a manipulative emotion that limits capacity growth and can trick us into living a boring life of disobedience. If the cure to physical paralysis is found in restoring messages between the brain and the muscles, the spiritual equivalent is simply restoring communication between the Head and the body.

Building our capacity to take healthy risks is found in the simplest of forms in Psalm 34:4 "I sought the LORD, and He answered me; He delivered me from all my fears..." He said it, I believe it and that settles it. As easy, and as difficult, as that.

Amazingly, once we start building our risk capacity we will soon discover the need to build our charitable capacity.

CHAPTER 10
Charitable Capacity
We need to customise our budget

To customise our budget is what Bishop Mark Dyer aptly called *"the recurring periods of 'rummage sales' in which we rid ourselves of what is no longer needed and rediscover treasures we have forgotten"*.

Once we've expanded our capacity for taking risks and we grow into new levels of trusting the Lord, it ultimately must reflect in our attitude towards our material possessions. There must be an expansion of our **CHARITABLE CAPACITY** if we want to grow and mature as believers.

I remember an incident with a good Dutch friend and colleague, Jan Pit, who was continually raising funds for the persecuted Church. He was once asked by a member of a Church he visited why he always preached so much about the "pocket" and so little about the "heart". Jan calmly looked at the gentleman and said: *"because it seems to me like most Christians have their hearts in their pockets."*

Over the past several years I have often listened to services where pastors mention the "fact" that the Bible talks more about "money" than hell (or any other topic for that matter). Usually there is a number associated with this bit of trivia – somewhere around 2,000 times. The point the pastors usually try to make is that God thinks money is a very important issue and it is usually tied to a sermon about tithing.

The truth is that God does think that money is important but not for the reasons we would assume. The first lie is that money is the most spoken about topic in the Bible. The one topic Jesus speaks more about than any other topic in the Gospels is the Kingdom of God. Jesus refers to kingdom of God or the Kingdom of Heaven or His Father's kingdom over 100 times in the Gospels compared to roughly 30 times where He speaks about money.

The second "unspoken truth" is that even though Jesus did speak a lot about money, it was mostly in a negative context. Some scriptural examples of Christ mentioning money can be found at:

- Matthew 6:19 *"Do not store up for yourselves treasures on earth, where moths and vermin destroy, and where thieves break in and steal."*
- Matthew 6:24 *"No one can serve two masters. Either you will hate the one and love the other, or you will be devoted to the one and despise the other. You cannot serve both God and money."*
- Matthew 10:9 *"Do not get any gold or silver or copper to take with you in your belts."*
- Matthew 22:21 *"Caesar's," they replied. Then he said to them, "So give back to Caesar what is Caesar's, and to God what is God's."*
- Mark 10:23 *Jesus looked around and said to his disciples, "How hard it is for the rich to enter the kingdom of God!"*
- Mark 10:25 *"It is easier for a camel to go through the eye of a needle than for someone who is rich to enter the kingdom of God."*
- Luke 1:53 *He has filled the hungry with good things but has sent the rich away empty.*
- Luke 18:25 *"Indeed, it is easier for a camel to go through the eye of a needle than for someone who is rich to enter the kingdom of God."*

The one reason why the Lord spoke often about money is not because of the value of money but because it reveals who we are. In Luke 18:18, 21a the Lord tells the rich man, *"If you wish to be complete, go and sell your possessions and give to the poor, and you will have treasure in heaven; and come, follow Me."* But when the young man heard this statement, he went away grieving (Luke 18:22-23a) and he went away "very sad, for he was extremely rich" (Luke 18:23b).

Scott Rodin writes, in his book *Stewards in the Kingdom: A Theology of Life in All Its Fullness* as follows:

"We must never for single moment lose sight of the stark realization that whenever we deal with money, we are dealing with dynamite. It is that, which the one day we control, and the next day becomes the controller. Such dynamite must be defused, and the greatest defuser that we as Christians have at our disposal is the opportunity to take that which seeks to dominate us and simply give it away. Think about it. There is not greater expression of money's total lack of dominance over us or of its low priority in our lives than when we can with joy and peace, give it away for the Lord's work. You cannot worship the God of mammon and be a free and cheerful giver. Likewise, you cannot serve the living God and be a hoarder of his resources. Giving, both how we give and how much we give, is the clearest outward expression of who our God really is. Our check stubs speak more honestly of our priorities than our church memberships."

Another book well worth reading is **Money, Possessions, and Eternity** by Randy Alcorn. Here are some quotes from a book that should be on the shelf of every believer. It addresses the spirit of building capacity by being charitable. Alcorn writes as follows:

What we do with our finances and resources in this life is our autobiography. Too often we assume that God has increased our income to increase our standard of living, when his stated purpose is to increase our standard of giving. (Look again at 2 Corinthians 8:14 and 9:11).

The antagonism between life and conscience may be removed either by a change of life or by a change of conscience. Many of us have elected to adjust our consciences rather than our lives. Our powers of rationalization are unlimited. They allow us to live in luxury and indifference while others, whom we could help if we chose to, starve and go to hell.

A disciple does not ask, "How much can I keep?" but, "How much more can I give?" Whenever we start to get comfortable with our level of giving, it's time to raise it again. Why would you not give? We err by beginning with the assumption that we should keep or spend the money God entrusts to us.

Giving should be the default choice. Unless there is a compelling reason to spend it or keep it, we should give it.

It's curious that the Church has become the most tightfisted at the very time in history when God has provided most generously. There's considerable talk about the end of the age, and many people seem to believe that Christ will return in their lifetime. But why is it that expecting Christ's return hasn't radically influenced our giving? Why is it that people who believe in the soon return of Christ are so quick to build their own financial empires--which prophecy tells us will perish--and so slow to build God's kingdom?

Shouldn't we just admit the obvious--that the New Testament call to discipleship, compassion, and giving leaves no room for the way many of us are thinking and living? Is it time to get beyond the theoretical stance of 'I'd be willing to give up anything if God asked me to,' and start actually giving up things in order to do what He's commanded us?

The words of Alcorn that struck me most were the following: *"Giving should be the default choice. Unless there is a compelling reason to spend it or keep it, we should give it."*

The questions are: when, why and how did we change the default settings of Christian charity? The instructions of the Lord was quite clear to anybody who would follow Him: (Mark 10:21) *"Go, sell everything you have and give to the poor, and you will have treasure in heaven. Then come, follow me."* The early Church made this the *modus operandi* of Church life and practised what Jesus preached. In Acts 4:33-35 we read how the apostles continued to testify with great power and that God's grace was powerfully at work in them all. The result was (34) *"that there were no needy persons among them. For from time to time those who owned land or houses sold them, brought the money from the sales and put it at the apostles' feet, and it was distributed to anyone who had need."*

They didn't decide what to keep and gave the rest away. They decided what to give away and the rest they kept. We have made "keeping" the default of our Christian walk instead of "giving". I meet so many Christians who ask the question whether our tithing should be based on our gross income or our net income. They just don't get it. It's not about the numbers, it's about the attitude.

So how do we expand our capacity to be more charitable? There are three dangers when pursuing this virtue:
- The first danger is pursuing wealth as a means to charity. This is like putting the cart in front of the horse.
- The second danger is expanding our capacity to give without pursuing justice. This is like having a cart without a horse.
- The third danger is expanding our charity as a sense of duty and not from a position of love. This is like having a horse without a cart.

PUTTING THE CART BEFORE THE HORSE

The relationship between charity and prosperity is abundantly clear in Scripture. Prosperity is a consequence of a selfless charitable life and not the condition for being generous. Seeking wealth in order to be charitable is therefore like putting the cart in front of the horse and becomes an upside-down pursuit of a Biblical virtue.

When meeting with a group of Syrian leaders during the devastating civil war that saw more than half the population uprooted and more than half a million killed, there was a spirit of charity among the believers that I have seldom experienced in such a tangible way. It was as if the leaders were all anointed with a baptism of charity that was harmoniously reflected in every testimony shared. The pastor from Aleppo shared how water wells were dug in all the Church compounds during a time of desperate water shortages and shared with everybody in the community. The leader from Homs shared how food parcels were distributed to hundreds of families who were trying to survive the devastation of war. These parcels were shared in times of personal shortages and had to be done across the "sniper line" where crossing the road could mean being shot by ISIS snipers. The pastor from Jaramana shared about their food programs every week to hundreds of families in an area where more than 13,000 bombs fell in a matter of five years.

All these provisions came in a time of no resources and little assistance. It was a time of tremendous capacity growth, shared the one pastor, and then provided the key : *"We learned that the key to experiencing God's provision is to give away what you want to keep."*

To expand our capacity to be more charitable will be one of the biggest virtue-builders that we can pursue. Think about these ten capacity building scriptures:

- *2 Corinthians 9:6 Whoever sows sparingly will also reap sparingly, and whoever sows generously will also reap generously.*
- *Proverbs 11:24,25 One person gives freely, yet gains even more; another withholds unduly, but comes to poverty. A generous person will prosper; whoever refreshes others will be refreshed.*
- *Proverbs 22:9 The generous will themselves be blessed, for they share their food with the poor.*
- *Deuteronomy 15:10 Give generously to them and do so without a grudging heart; then because of this the LORD your God will bless you in all your work and in everything you put your hand to.*
- *Psalm 112:5 Good will come to those who are generous and lend freely, who conduct their affairs with justice.*
- *Psalm 112:9 They have freely scattered their gifts to the poor, their righteousness endures forever; their horn will be lifted high in honor.*
- *1Timothy 6:18 Command them to do good, to be rich in good deeds, and to be generous and willing to share.*
- *1Timothy 6:19 In this way they will lay up treasure for themselves as a firm foundation for the coming age, so that they may take hold of the life that is truly life.*
- *Luke 6:38 Give, and it will be given to you. A good measure, pressed down, shaken together and running over, will be poured into your lap. For with the measure you use, it will be measured to you.*

And my personal favourite
- *Proverbs 19:17 Whoever is kind to the poor lends to the LORD, and he will reward them for what they have done.*

Who in his right mind would not lend to the Lord as much as possible? Who would not desire to invest in eternity beyond their current capacity?

So let's not confuse the issue of wealth and charity, or even the fact that we need the one to fulfil the other. Of course we all know that money as a means is not evil, but money as a goal is. Having money is not evil but we are taught that **the love of money** is the foundation of all that is evil (1Timothy 6:8-10)[95]. Money is a wonderful servant, but a terrible master.

This chapter is therefore not about the capacity to gather, but to share, not to gain, but to lose. It is not about riches, but about charity

HAVING A CART WITHOUT THE HORSE

The second danger in expanding our capacity to be charitable is that we focus only on half of the virtue. The important component of charity that is often missed, or neglected, when taught from pulpits and in seminars, is the virtue of justice. Pursuing charity without justice is like sitting in a cart without having a horse to pull it.

Expanding our capacity in the joint virtues of charity and justice combined, should be one of the first priorities in the life of every follower of Christ. This is not de-prioritising prayer and worship or even demoting our times of silence before the Lord and of going to Church. These two virtues are actually the expressions of our spiritual acts of prayer and worship. We need to re-evaluate the core of the Christian life and seek to expand those

---

[95] 1Timothy 6:8-10 – But if we have food and clothing, we will be content with that. People who want to get rich fall into temptation and a trap and into many foolish and harmful desires that plunge men into ruin and destruction. For the love of money is a root of all kinds of evil. Some people, eager for money, have wandered from the faith and pierced themselves with many griefs.

capacities before pursuing anything else. And when we are tempted to think charity and justice are secondary to a life of prayer, worship, Bible readings and quiet times, and that our focus should be more on the Kingdom of Heaven not on the things of this world, perhaps we should listen to God Himself in Isaiah 58 where we find the connection between worship, fasting, prayer, and the expression of charity and justice:

Isaiah 58:5-7 "Is this the kind of fast I have chosen, only a day for people to humble themselves? Is it only for bowing one's head like a reed and for lying in sackcloth and ashes? Is that what you call a fast, a day acceptable to the LORD? Is not this the kind of fasting I have chosen: to loose the chains of injustice and untie the cords of the yoke, to set the oppressed free and break every yoke? Is it not to share your food with the hungry and to provide the poor wanderer with shelter— when you see the naked, to clothe them, and not to turn away from your own flesh and blood?"

This Scripture gives us a stark warning that when we fail to develop acts of charity and justice we are in danger of staying spiritual infants even though we might have the outward appearance of being super spiritual, praying powerful prayers and having wonderful worship. We might have a beautifully decorated cart that we sit in, but without a horse we will still be going nowhere.

Isaiah speaks here the "personal" words of God Himself, not as a theology to discuss but as a mandate for action. He addresses the two linked virtues of justice and charity. When he speaks of setting people free from the "chains of injustice" he is speaking of justice and then when he speaks of sharing bread with the hungry, sheltering the homeless, etc., he is speaking of charity.

What Isaiah is saying is that our religious rituals – going to church, reading our Bible, prayers and worship – are not ends in themselves. Our religious activities are designed to put us in the presence of God to be transformed, so that we might have that "mind in us" that is in Jesus, as Paul tells us. It is in our attempts to love ourselves and others that we truly meet the Lord.

There are more examples in Scripture and this message was quite clear from a number of ancient prophets who spoke the words of God. Remember Amos and Micah. Speaking for the Lord, Amos said:

(Amos 5:21-24) *"I hate, I despise your religious festivals; your assemblies are a stench to me. Even though you bring me burnt offerings and grain offerings, I will not accept them. Though you bring choice fellowship offerings, I will have no regard for them. Away with the noise of your songs! I will not listen to the music of your harps. But let justice roll on like a river, righteousness like a never-failing stream!"*

Micah was equally blunt:

(Micah 6:6-8) *"With what shall I come before the LORD and bow down before the exalted God? Shall I come before him with burnt offerings, with calves a year old? Will the LORD be pleased with thousands of rams, with ten thousand rivers of olive oil? Shall I offer my firstborn for my transgression, the fruit of my body for the sin of my soul? He has shown you, O mortal, what is good. And what does the LORD require of you? To act justly and to love mercy and to walk humbly with your God."*

Amos and Micah lived in the 8th century BC. This was a time of peace and prosperity in Israel. However, most of the fruits of prosperity were enjoyed only by the upper class, who assumed that simply because they performed the cultic rituals, God was pleased with them and thus granted them prosperity and peace. They saw no need for social justice. However, Amos and Micah spoke out against social injustice. The poor had to sell themselves to get out of small debts, the rich falsified the weights and measures and the courts were corrupt. Amos and Micah were not against the cults as such, but in the way they were practised. They declared that doing the will of God in the holy place must conform to doing the will of God in the marketplace. The essence of a true spirituality is to put ourselves in the presence of God, i.e., going to church on Sunday, reading our Bibles, religious discussion groups, meditation etc., so that we can be transformed by that experience and go on to lead a life dedicated to love of self, others, the world and our God.

We even find the ultimate example of justice and charity from God Himself in John 3:16 where God so loved the world (charity) that He gave His only begotten Son so that whoever believes in Him will not perish but have everlasting life (justice).

If God sent Christ to earth as judge there would be no difference between Christianity, Islam, Hinduism or even Judaism. Jesus did not come to judge but to secure justice[96]. He was a gift of charity to a world that is incapable of standing righteous before God, holy and just. But at the same time charity without justice would not reflect the character of God. God is righteous and just and all will, and must, be judged according to His Word. But charity provides an immediate answer for an eternal need.

What is the difference between Charity and Justice? Charles Dickens perhaps summed it up best with his quote that charity begins at home but justice begins next door. Ralph Nader explained that a society that has more justice is a society that needs less charity. Both these quotes provide a good understanding of how these two virtues are linked together. But one of the better elaborated explanations is found on the website of St Marys: http://sites.saintmarys.edu/~incandel/charjust.html

CHARITY	JUSTICE
Charity equals social **service**.	Justice equals social **change**.
Charity provides direct services like food, clothing, shelter.	Justice promotes social change in institutions or political structures.
Charity responds to **immediate needs**.	Justice responds to **long-term needs**.
Charity is directed at the **effects of injustice**, its symptoms	Justice is **directed at the root causes** of social problems.

[96] John 12:47 "If anyone hears my words but does not keep them, I do not judge that person. For I did not come to judge the world, but to save the world."

CHARITY	JUSTICE
Charity addresses problems that already exist. Otherwise put: **LOVE MOPS UP.**	Justice addresses the underlying structures or causes of these problems. Otherwise put: **JUSTICE TRIES TO MAKE SURE THE MESS ISN'T MADE TO BEGIN WITH.**
Charity is **private**, individual acts.	Justice is **public**, collective actions.
Examples of charity: homeless shelters, food shelves, clothing drives, emergency services.	Examples of justice: legislative advocacy, changing policies and practices, political action.

Perhaps the best way to differentiate between two often-confused terms is to re-tell the parable revolving around these two concepts:
There was a village holding a social gathering one summer, when a person noticed a baby struggling and crying in the river. As someone rushed to save the baby, more babies appeared, so the people tried saving the children. As others became busy with their rescue efforts, two people went upstream to stop whoever was throwing the babies into the river.

This may seem to be an improbable tale, but the difference between the concepts of justice and charity are clearly outlined. Charity occurred when the townspeople put their efforts together to rescue the babies, while justice was sought by the two individuals who went upstream to stop whoever was throwing the babies downstream.

Expanding and building our capacity to be charitable will require involvement both **IN** the river and also **UP** the river.

HAVING A HORSE WITHOUT A CART

The third danger in expanding our capacity to be charitable is that we give either from a sense of guilt or a sense of duty. We might think we have the right motives and our intentions might be pure in helping those in need but the vehicle needed to "transport" our actions is missing. Good intentions are just not good enough anymore. We need to move into a new dimension when we contemplate charity; away from a deep sense of guilt as to why I have so much and others so little; away from a sense of duty that this is what the Bible demands of those who follow Christ.

Jesus is known as the Father of all compassion[97]. He does charity because of who He is, not because He needs to. He doesn't love out of duty but because He cannot NOT do it. His divine character is to save, to help, to love. It is not only reflected in His nature but also in His name: JESHUA – HE SAVES.

And because we have Christ in us, this becomes our DNA as well and as Christians we expand this capacity not because we believe in Jesus but because He is IN us. We cannot NOT be charitable. The only thing that counts in the life of a believer is faith expressing itself through love. At least that's what Galatians 5:6 says[98]

One of the best descriptions I found of why Christians should pursue charity in relation to Galatians 5:6 was written by Richard Rohr. He wrote as follows:

"Beloved, let us love one another, because love is from God; everyone who loves is born of God and knows God. Whoever does not love does not know God, for God is love. . . . No one has ever seen God; if we love one another, God lives in us, and [God's] love is perfected in us. —1 John 4:7-8, 12

"In light of Scriptures like these (and Galatians 5:6), you might think that the primacy of love would be a settled matter in Christian faith. But here we are two thousand years into this religion, and for many beliefs still rule, and love

---

[97] 2 Corinthians 1:3-4 Praise be to the God and Father of our Lord Jesus Christ, the Father of compassion and the God of all comfort, who comforts us in all our troubles, so that we can comfort those in any trouble with the comfort we ourselves receive from God.

[98] Galatians 5:6 For in Christ Jesus neither circumcision nor uncircumcision has any value. The only thing that counts is faith expressing itself through love.

too often waits out in the hallway, hoping to be invited in and taken more seriously. True, we may have decentered old behavior-correctness codes, but in essence, many of us have merely exchanged them for new belief-correctness codes. We couldn't handle the call to faith expressing itself in love, so we reverted to beliefs expressing themselves in exclusion instead.

". . . If Christian faith can be redefined in this way, if our prime contribution to humanity can be shifted from teaching correct beliefs to practicing the way of love as Jesus taught, then our whole understanding and experience of the church could be transformed . . . [into] a school of love.

"What I believe can and should happen is that tens of thousands of congregations will become what I call "schools" or "studios" of love. . . . What I care about is whether they are teaching people to live a life of love, from the heart, for God, for all people (no exceptions), and for all creation. . . .

"If our churches make this migration, if they make the way of love their highest aim, they will experience what Paul prayed for in his Epistle to the Ephesians: their members will be "strengthened in [their] inner being with power through [God's] Spirit, [so] that Christ may dwell in [their] hearts through faith, as [they] are being rooted and grounded in love" (3:16-17). They will employ every text, prayer, song, poem, work of visual and dramatic art, ritual, rite of passage, and other spiritual resource to help people comprehend "what is the breadth and length and height and depth, and to know the love of Christ that surpasses knowledge, so that [they] may be filled with all the fullness of God" (3:18-19)."

GOLD OR IRON?

When we as followers of Christ pursue the virtue of charity, we're invited to exchange material excesses and earthly possessions for a Kingdom reward.

There is a wonderful piece of history recorded of King Frederick William III of Prussia. King Frederick was king of Prussia from 1797 to 1840. He ruled Prussia during the difficult times of the Napoleonic Wars and the end of the Holy Roman Empire. King Frederick found himself in crippling debt during his reign because of the war efforts. As he sought to build his nation, finances had simply run out. His loyal long-suffering subjects trusted him to provide for them, but he felt cornered. Capitulation to the enemy was unthinkable, but what else could he do? In the end, he devised a creative plan. He asked all the women of Prussia to bring their gold and silver jewellery to be melted down for King and country. As a replacement for each ornament, they would receive a bronze or iron decoration as a symbol of gratitude. Each insignia had inscribed: "I gave gold for iron. 1813." He could not have anticipated the overwhelming response that followed. Most women prized their gifts from the king much more highly than their former jewellery. The reason why became quickly apparent. The insignias were proof that they had sacrificed for their king. In due course, it actually became fashionable to wear them as jewellery. Thus was established the Order of the Iron Cross. Members wore no ornaments except a cross of iron for all to see.

When we as followers of Christ come to our King, we're invited likewise to exchange material excesses and adornments for a cross. Of course jewellery is not wrong in itself, but as the women of Prussia discovered with joy when offered the chance to sacrifice for the King, laying down our valued possessions for a greater cause is so much more worthwhile. As John Piper wrote: "God is calling us to be conduits of His grace, not cul-de-sacs. Our great danger today is thinking that the conduit should be lined with gold. It shouldn't. Copper will do. No matter how grateful we are, gold will not make the world think that our God is good; it will make people think that our god is gold."

Amazingly, once we start building our charitable capacity we will soon discover the need to build our BEHAVIOURAL capacity.

CHAPTER 11
Behavioural Capacity
We need to restructure our actions

As with works of charity and working toward justice, changing our behaviour accordingly is no small task. It will demand a great deal from us. There must therefore be an expansion of our **BEHAVIOURAL CAPACITY** if we want to grow and mature as believers.

But, and this is key in understanding how our actions are tangible expressions of our faith, we do not devote ourselves to DOING good **TO BE** saved, we devote ourselves to DOING good **BECAUSE** we are saved. We do not devote ourselves to LOVE **TO OBTAIN** the love of God, we devote ourselves to LOVE **BECAUSE** we have obtained the love of God. And we will only truly understand this principle once we realise that our actions become a transactional **"currency"** of our faith. Whatever we hope to obtain spiritually will be determined by the currency we use.

I experienced the practical application of this Biblical truth during a visit to America when I accidentally produced a South African R2.00 coin while trying to pay for a cup of coffee at a local restaurant. Roughly the same size and colour as a US Quarter, the waiter did not spot the inconsistency immediately, but it did not take her long to return with the faulty coin. ***"Sorry sir, with this currency you cannot buy that product,"*** the lady said with a smile and pointed simultaneously to the coin and the coffee.

My thoughts immediately went back to a conversation I had on Facebook with a mission leader who kept on using pictures and messages of crime in South Africa to inform believers of the corruption and violence in the nation. The specific post that led to our conversation had a picture of the new president, Mr.Cyril Ramaphosa, and an alleged report of his intentions to turn South Africa into a next Zimbabwe.

"Why sow suspicion and fear in a time of hope?" was my question to him. His response was short and simple: *"Thanks for your feedback. But I don't see it as sowing fear, I see it as standing up for the truth"*

"Sorry sir, with that currency you cannot buy that product."

The product we hope to obtain might be noble and Biblical but no virtue can be obtained through unbiblical attitudes and actions. Remember this, with a carnal currency (fear, suspicion, slander and gossip) we can't buy a Kingdom product (peace, truth, reconciliation and love).

In order to expand our behavioural capacity we need to focus more on the **"currency"** of our actions than the **"product"** we hope to obtain.

Listen to Galatians 5:16-23: *So I say, walk by the Spirit, and you will not gratify the desires of the flesh. For the flesh desires what is contrary to the Spirit, and the Spirit what is contrary to the flesh. They are in conflict with each other, so that you are not to do whatever you want. But if you are led by the Spirit, you are not under the law. The acts of the flesh are obvious: sexual immorality, impurity and debauchery; idolatry and witchcraft; hatred, discord, jealousy, fits of rage, selfish ambition, dissensions, factions and envy; drunkenness, orgies, and the like. I warn you, as I did before, that those who live like this will not inherit the kingdom of God. But the fruit of the Spirit is love, joy, peace, forbearance, kindness, goodness, faithfulness, gentleness and self-control. Against such things there is no law.*

What Galatians 3 in effect teaches us is that currencies "of the flesh" cannot buy products "of the Spirit" .
- The currency of jealousy will buy suspicion
- The currency of suspicion will buy division
- The currency of division will buy fear
- The currency of fear will buy hatred
- The currency of hatred will buy anger
- The currency of anger will buy war

- The currency of war will buy destruction

These currencies may secure our kingdoms on earth, our safety and our security, but it will exclude us from an eternal Kingdom. The only currency we can deal with as Christians, no matter how noble the intention, is to deal in a currency that belong to the Kingdom of Heaven.
- The currency of love will buy harmony
- The currency of harmony will buy forbearance
- The currency of forbearance will buy restraint
- The currency of restraint will buy truth
- The currency of truth will buy kindness, goodness and gentleness
- The currency of kindness, goodness and gentleness will buy peace

How do we therefore approach the daunting task of aligning **"product"** to **"currency"** and dealing in a way that will reflect our alliance to the Kingdom of Heaven? It will involve seven transformations:
- From horse to hawk
- From surprise to surrender
- From admiration to activation
- From duty to delight
- From the mundane to the momentous
- From relaxed to resolved
- From obligation to opportunity

FROM HORSE TO HAWK

*Ephesians 5:15-16 See then that ye walk circumspectly, not as fools, but as wise, **redeeming the time**, because the days are evil. (KJV)*

Visiting a friend recently, I enthusiastically shared how I saved 10 minutes of the journey by taking a shorter route. My friend looked at me with a smile and simply asked, *"What are you going to do with it?"* That was a very legitimate question. Time is a precious and an irreplaceable commodity. It is the only product that we cannot save or keep for later use; once it's gone, it's gone. The question is: what do we do with it?

One of the concepts featuring most in Scripture is the concept of *TIME*. The actual word "time" appears in 713 verses in the Bible (NIV), nearly twice as much as the word "sin".

But is time tangible or is it an illusion?

Albert Einstein concluded in his "Theory of Relativism" that the past, present, and future all exist at the same time and rejected the notion that the past and future are divided by the "now".   He believed in a "single existence" which he based on the idea that one person in a spaceship, travelling across various date lines, is able to experience several days while another person on earth simultaneously experiences only a few hours or minutes. The same two people can meet up again, one having experienced days or even years while the other has only experienced hours and days. If those in the spaceship are able to travel at the speed of light, their time would cease completely, and they would only exist trapped in timelessness.

This reminded me of meeting a friend in the USA who had just arrived from New Zealand. *"When did you leave Auckland?"* I asked. *"Oh, I am actually only leaving in an hour's time,"* he replied. He obviously flew back across the date-line and even though he flew for a number of hours he was still ahead of time.   It was quite sobering to know that he had already experienced something of the day in time that we had not even entered yet.

According to this concept of time it appears that time is more a direction in space than a moment in history. This becomes quite significant in our endeavours to use our time wisely and to be good stewards of it. We can so easily miss the wisdom of the Bible when we end up running headlong down a path that we think is correct, but we just get further away from where we should be. In understanding that God is timeless it becomes so much more critical to understand His perspective on this precious commodity.

Time is probably one of the most precious gifts entrusted to any human being. We are told to…:

- **USE IT:** *Esther 4:14 … And who knows but that you have come to your royal position for such a time as this?*
- **APPRECIATE IT**: *Ecclesiastes 3:11 He has made everything beautiful in its time. He has also set eternity in the human heart; yet no one can fathom what God has done from beginning to end.*
- **NUMBER IT:** *Psalm 90:12 Teach us to number our days, that we may gain a heart of wisdom.*
- **MANAGE IT:** *John 9:4 As long as it is day, we must do the works of him who sent me. Night is coming, when no one can work.*
- **REDEEM IT**: *Colossians 4:5 Walk in wisdom toward them that are without, redeeming the time. (KJV)*

But to use time wisely we are probably best advised to

- **RESCUE IT:** *Ephesians 5:15-16 See then that ye walk circumspectly, not as fools, but as wise, redeeming the time, because the days are evil.*

The word used for *REDEEM in this verse* is *ex-ag-or-ad'-zo;* literally to "buy up, to rescue or to redeem". The word for *TIME* is *kahee-ros',* literally "an *OPPORTUNITY*, or due season". Ephesians 5:16 uses a metaphor taken from merchants and traders who diligently observed and improved the seasons for merchandise and trade. As Christians we are called to seize what the season offers and save what would otherwise be lost.

On his blog, *Life of a Steward*[99], Loren Pinilis explores Ephesians 5:15-16 by comparing effective time stewardship with a horse with blinders who ploughs the ground for hours and hours every day, or like the hawk whose sharp senses are scanning the area.

---

[99] http://www.lifeofasteward.com/chronos-kairos/

The two Greek words most frequently used for "time" in the new Testament are *khron'-os* (chronos) and *kahee-ros* (Kairos). Both words mean time, but they imply two completely different concepts.

Chronos, as found in Galatians 4:4[100], refers to the minutes and the hours we so preciously ration every day. It is time as a measurable resource that points to a direction. Kairos on the other hand, as used in Ephesians 5:16[101], refers to a season or an appointed time. It is a moment of time that points to an opportunity.

Pinilis explains as follows:
"THE CHRONOS OUTLOOK: *We tend to think of our time in a chronos mindset. We think of having 24 hours in a day. We define our workweeks by the number of hours that we work. We have a list of things to do and only so much time to get everything done.*

"Being conscious of our minutes and seconds is a good thing. We should number our days as the scripture says. Our time on earth is so brief, and we want to be good stewards of every second that we have to glorify God on this earth. But ironically, this chronos mindset can make us miss what Paul is saying in Ephesians 5. Paul instructs us to redeem the kairos — to pay attention and take advantage of the opportune times and seasons.

A KAIROS VIEW: *We only have such a brief opportunity to shepherd our kids when they're still young children. When a friend is experiencing pain, we have a brief window of time in which to reach out to them. When we contemplate global events and witness millions of refugees seeking hope and dignity, we are presented with a Kairos moment in history. Yes, it will require some of our chronos time. But this kairos opportunity will have a "sell-by-date" and once it's gone, it will be gone*

---

[100] Galatians 4:4 But when the set time had fully come, God sent his Son, born of a woman, born under the law,

[101] Ephesians 5:15-16 See then that ye walk circumspectly, not as fools, but as wise, Redeeming the time, because the days are evil.

CHANGING OUR MINDSET

This requires us to make a mental shift. Instead of looking at our time as grains of sand slipping through an hourglass, we view our time as opportunities flying by. Instead of viewing our time as seconds ticking by, we realize that not every second holds the same worth. Some moments are more valuable than other moments. The five minutes that I have a chance to share the gospel with an unsaved friend is a more valuable five minutes than when I'm processing my Email. I have to take advantage of my opportunities.

We must change our view of what effectiveness really is. Though we want to use our minutes and seconds wisely, biblical effectiveness is not necessarily us ramming as much as we can into 24 hours. It's not us putting our head down and ploughing the field with as much vigour as we can muster.

Instead the effective steward is a focused watchman whose senses are attuned to the slightest hint of an opportunity. He's a hawk on the lookout. The effective steward not only recognizes these kairos opportunities but has the courage to leap upon them with all his might. And the effective steward has organized his schedule in such a way that leaves him open to seizing these opportunities.

Don't let your diligence towards chronos choke out your attention to kairos. Don't count your years (chronos), make your years count (Kairos).

Are you a horse or a hawk?

FROM SURPRISE TO SURRENDER

One of the best guidelines that I ever came across of expanding our behavioural capacity comes from the pen of Richard Rohr. This might at first seem like too deep a philosophical approach, but read it a few times and understand the Biblical value of finding ourselves in the surprise and the surrender of each moment we encounter. This will open new doors to a journey that we seldom understand when trotting through life like every moment is just a mirror of the previous one. Richard Rohr writes as follows:

To begin to see with new eyes, we must observe—and usually be humiliated by—the habitual way we encounter each and every moment. It is humiliating because we will see that we are well-practiced in just a few predictable responses. Not many of our responses are original, fresh, or naturally respectful of what is right in front of us. The most common human responses to a new moment are mistrust, cynicism, fear, defensiveness, dismissal, and judgmentalism. These are the common ways the ego tries to be in control of the data instead of allowing the moment to get some control over us—and teach us something new!

To let the moment teach us, we must allow ourselves to be at least slightly surprised by it until it draws us inward and upward, toward a subtle experience of wonder. We normally need a single moment of gratuitous awe to get us started. Look, for example, at the Exodus narrative: It all begins with a murderer (Moses) on the run from the law, encountering a paradoxical bush that "burns without being consumed." Awestruck, he takes off his shoes and the very earth beneath his feet becomes "holy ground" (see Exodus 3:2-6) because he has met "the Great I Am" (Exodus 3:14[102]). This narrative reveals the classic pattern, repeated in different forms in the varied lives and vocabulary of all the world's saints.

The spiritual journey is a constant interplay between moments of surprise followed by a process of surrender to that moment. We must first allow ourselves to be captured by the goodness, truth, or beauty of something beyond and outside ourselves. Then we universalize from that moment to the goodness, truth, and beauty of the rest of reality, until our realization eventually ricochets back to include ourselves! This is the great inner dialogue we call prayer. We humans resist both the awe and, even more, the surrender. Both are vital, and so we must practice.

---

[102] Exodus 3:14 God said to Moses, "I AM WHO I AM. This is what you are to say to the Israelites: 'I AM has sent me to you.'"

The way to any universal idea is to proceed through a concrete encounter. The one is the way to the many; the specific is the way to the spacious; the now is the way to the always; the here is the way to everywhere; the material is the way to the spiritual; the visible is the way to the invisible. When we see contemplatively, we know that we live in a fully sacramental universe, where everything is an epiphany.

While philosophers tend toward universals and poets love particulars, mystics and contemplative practice teach us how to encompass both.

So, to proceed in expanding our behavioural capacity we need to identify every moment as a divine opportunity to be awe struck and then surrender. Just like Moses did.

FROM ADMIRATION TO ACTIVATION

There is a misconception among Christians that being good is good enough. Well, it isn't. **Being** good needs to translate into **doing** good. God's call to holiness is not only about not doing sin, it's about being set apart for good works[103].

The danger is that if we view our default position in Christ as **the commission of omission** it will result in **the omission of the commission**. In other words, if we believe that the instruction (commission) in Scripture is simply withholding (omission) from "doing wrong things", then we ultimately neglect the instructions of the Lord to act and put feet to our faith. We all find it a lot easier not doing to others what we don't want done to ourselves than it is doing unto others what we want done to ourselves. But according to Matthew 7:12[104] to **"DO"** sums up the law and the

---

[103] Ephesians 2:10 For we are God's handiwork, created in Christ Jesus to do good works, which God prepared in advance for us to do.

[104] Matthew 7:12 So in everything, do to others what you would have them do to you, for this sums up the Law and the Prophets.

prophets. This is not a call to devotion but to action. It's far easier omitting the bad than committing to the good. This was the call of Christ to holiness.

Our devotion and "holy admiration" of God need to translate into doing and a "wholly activation" for God

Benjamin Franklin is reported to have said, *"If you want something done, give it to a busy person."*

This is more than just a good quote. Many leaders will testify that this principle is very often the life-line of an effective team. There's a reason why busy people are busy, and people with time to waste have time to waste. Find the busiest member of the team for the odd urgent job, and you know it will be done.

If you do a Google search to find some answers from the experts as to why this is actually a proven fact, there are a number of logical explanations: One explanation is that people who get more done are usually well-organized. They prioritize, they make tough calls, they delegate, they plan their routes, and they are effective. You can give them something extra to do, then watch them recalculate their workload to adjust. They also ask smart questions: why, when, how, what's more important? And sometimes even "can it happen tomorrow?" because often that task will slot more perfectly into the next day's schedule. Essentially, they make the most of their time. This is true!

But there is another reason why busy people are more effective in taking more responsibilities than those who are simply getting by in their daily tasks. It is because busy people have already expanded their capacity to do more.

We live in a season where believers need to expand their behavioural capacity like never before. There needs to be a new urgency in the hearts of those who follow Christ. Without expanding our capacity to DO we run the risk of becoming the most obese Christian generation of all time. There also exists the real danger that we could be the first Christian generation that is entertained to death.

"Our people must learn to devote themselves to DOING what is good," are the words of Titus to the Church[105] - *"in order to provide for the urgent needs and not live unproductive lives."* Productivity is found in doing, as a hallmark of our devotion. Sadly, we have taken the combination of DEVOTION and DOING and turned it into DEVOTION and TALKING. It became a quick early morning Scripture reading, a short message and a quick prayer. It became Morning Devotions instead of Daily Activities. According to the "Titus devotion", urgency, capacity, proactive lives and productivity are closely connected to one another.

Many Christians find their spiritual identity in their quiet times and focus their entire spirituality on being still and "hearing from the Lord". This is obviously an important component in the life of every believer and might develop spiritual capacity but in a contradistinctive context, without adding the virtue of labour, will produce unbalanced Christians. We are both called to make *the most of every opportunity*[106] as well as *to be still, and know that He is God*[107]. Both capacities need to be expanded and sadly many believers are often *"so heavenly minded that they are no earthly good"*. As cricketer turned pioneer missionary, C. T. Studd, declared: **"You only have one life, it will soon be past. Only what's done for Christ will last!"**

In order to expand our behavioural capacity we have to change our ADMIRATION into ACTIVATION. We have to put feet to our faith.

---

[105] Titus 3:14 Our people must learn to devote themselves to doing what is good, in order to provide for urgent needs and not live unproductive lives.

[106] Ephesians 5:16: making the most of every opportunity, because the days are evil.

[107] Psalm 46:10 He says, "Be still, and know that I am God; I will be exalted among the nations, I will be exalted in the earth."

FROM DUTY TO DELIGHT

It is equally true that while some believers misinterpret devotion as "quiet time", others interpret devotion as duty. We do missions because the Bible teaches us to go to the ends of the earth. We pursue holiness because Christ commanded us to do so. We live charitable lives because "it is the right thing to do". This is not wrong and neither is it bad but behaviour that is driven by duty will never create the space for capacity growth. I love the quote that says *Life (faith) is best for those who are enjoying it. Difficult for those who are analyzing it and worse for those who are criticizing it. Our attitude defines our life and is inclusive of all good as well.*

I remember my first visit to Egypt nearly 30 years ago as if it was yesterday. It was my first exposure to the persecuted Church in the Middle East and I was expecting a spiritually strong, serious and duty-bound Church that bore the marks of the cross. I found this, but I found more, much much more.

I found believers that shared the utter delight of sharing the cross of Christ and a joy that I had not seen before. We met this strange leader who was to become like a twin brother to me; Magdy Saber and his wife Annelise. They invited us into their home and they welcomed us into their lives but most of all, they introduced us into a new attitude of doing ministry. I experienced a delight that challenged my behavioural capacity like few encounters in the past.

And, thinking back to nearly thirty years of serving the persecuted Church, if I have to draw a picture to embody all my encounters it will be that of a smiling face. Not a smile of happiness because, believe me, there are not always reasons to be happy. Not even a smile of joy, even though the joy of the Lord is always their strength. But a smile of pure delight! And there is a huge difference:
- Happiness is a feeling[108]

---

[108] James_5:13 Is anyone among you in trouble? Let them pray. Is anyone happy? Let them sing songs of praise.

- Joy is an attitude[109]
- Delight is an expression[110]

In order to expand our behavioural capacity we have to move from DUTY to DELIGHT

A few years ago we were invited as a South African team to go to Switzerland. I found it difficult, to say the least. You see, one of my major misconceptions in my first 23 years of ministry was that service is only meaningful in God's Kingdom if it is ministry related. Please read this carefully.

I firmly believed that my gratitude to the Lord for His grace and mercy can only be showed by how much I am willing to sacrifice for Him. Which in a sense is true, but not the whole truth. I believed and practised the saying that *"the price of anything is the amount of life you are willing to exchange for it".*

Something in Switzerland expanded my capacity. I found a new delight in what God had given us as a team. Not only a joy in what we were doing but a joy in the Giver. I discovered that being "delighted" in His goodness was as much part of my service as my "doing" in His service. I came to an understanding that the greatest way that I can show my gratitude to the Lord is by enjoying every opportunity He allows in my life to recognize Him as the Lord of my life. Whether this be in a mud shack in Sudan, the slums of India or the villa in Switzerland. I realised my devotion, my doing and my duty all needed to accumulate into pure delight.

Delight is the reason why Paul so boldly proclaimed that he had learned to be content whatever the circumstances, in need and in plenty[111]. I found

---

[109] Nehemiah 8:10 … Do not grieve, for the joy of the LORD is your strength."

[110] Psalm 37:4 Take delight in the LORD, and he will give you the desires of your heart.

[111] Philippians 4:11-12 I am not saying this because I am in need, for I have learned to be content whatever the circumstances. I know what it is to be in need, and I know what it is to have plenty. I

that this expression of delight, opposed to duty, is what the Lord desires and increases capacity in four ways:

1. DELIGHT increases our field of inspiration
Taste and see that the Lord is good. (Psalm 34:8)
Delight really is the ability to enjoy joy – to have pleasure in what God allows us to enjoy.

2. DELIGHT increases our image of God
Another theological misunderstanding I often nurtured in my life as a missionary was the thought that God was mostly concerned about my missional achievements and less about my missional enjoyments.
This verse changed my mind...
Bad as you are, you know how to give good things to your children. How much more, then, will your Father in heaven give good things to those who ask him! (Matthew 7:11)

3. DELIGHT increases our Capacity to enjoy life
Joh 10:10 The thief comes only to steal and kill and destroy; I have come that they may have life, and have it to the full.
Jolly is not folly. God isn't only good to you, He also wants you to enjoy His goodness. God gives us all things freely to enjoy.
If God gives a man wealth and property and lets him enjoy them, he should be grateful and enjoy what he has worked for. It is a gift from God. (Ecclesiastes 5:19)
Did you notice? The words "grateful" and "enjoy" happen at the same time.

4. DELIGHT increases our efforts to return His goodness
Psalm 116:12-14 What shall I return to the LORD for all his goodness to me? I will lift up the cup of salvation and call on the name of the LORD. I will fulfill my vows to the LORD in the presence of all his people.

---

have learned the secret of being content in any and every situation, whether well fed or hungry, whether living in plenty or in want.

We make a living by what we get, we make a life by what we give.
— *Winston Churchill*

FROM THE MUNDANE TO THE MOMENTOUS

I read a sermon on the internet recently (for this one I would prefer not to provide the source) of a pastor who asks this question: *"Does church bore you?"* He himself then confesses that before he had to plan worship services, come up to the front and preach and lead all the different aspects of the worship service, he too would say that church bored him. As encouragement he then affirms that **we are allowed to** be bored by church sometimes. He then concludes with these words ***"But shouldn't we be okay with it if every single worship service doesn't get our blood flowing. We can't be on a spiritual high all the time."***

Oh, may the Lord have mercy on us. We have exchanged our momentous daily encounters as we journey with Christ, like sheep among the wolves, and seeing miracles and wonders as daily events, into a boring, sceptical Sunday faith. And worst of all, we are content with it and find it acceptable. We might find our delight in the Lord but still continue to sit in the same pew Sunday after Sunday in doing that.

No, I'm not going to make you feel good about being bored. If you are, then you are the one to blame, not your faith, and most of all not God. God the Creator, miracle worker, Saviour of souls, the One who separated the oceans and made time stand still, the One who healed the sick and raised the dead, this God is not a boring God. Following Him can only become boring when we settle into behavioural habits; good habits maybe but nonetheless behavioural habits that lead to death. According to Wikipedia habits are automatic routines of behaviour that are repeated regularly, without thinking. They are learned, not instinctive, human behaviours that occur automatically, without the explicit contemporaneous intention of the person.

The one sure test to see if you have stagnated in your behavioural capacity is to ask this simple question: *Is my faith habitual?* In other words, do I do what I do because I am used to doing what I do. Do I go to Church Sunday after Sunday, and Bible studies on Wednesdays, because that is the way it's done? If the answer is yes or even "from time to time" then you are in desperate need to expand your behavioural capacity.

As parents, my wife and I have made many mistakes in raising our children, but one of the better decisions we have made was taking them with us whenever we travelled to the persecuted Church. They grew up with a deep understanding that Christianity is extravagantly momentous. Elisha and Helga were eight and six years old respectively when they smuggled Bibles into Russia for the first time. They travelled with us when we encouraged the Church in Romania, sitting with us when we did training in Egypt, travelling with when we delivered material in Vietnam, sharing in the needs of believers in China, weeping with us in the Middle East and encountering heroes of faith in Asia.

Faith might have cost them the comforts of life and even the absence at times of parents, but never robbed them of the adventures that few others of their age experienced.

You will rediscover a momentous Christian life again by …
- Skipping Church one Sunday morning and visiting the hospital to BE church
- Skipping prayer meetings at Church one evening to go and pray for someone who needs a touch of prayer more than a word of prayer
- Skipping holidays one year and volunteering for an outreach to a needy area nearby or across the borders
- Skipping the annual missions conference to go to the missions field

But be warned, a taste of the momentous God we serve will leave you breathless and totally discontent with the mundane. This will not only create a desire to "taste more" but also thrust you out of the complacency into the urgent.

FROM RELAXED TO RESOLVED

It is true, as Jim Rohn rightly proclaimed, that *"without a sense of urgency, desire loses its value"*. This applies to the spiritual life of every believer. If we lose the sense of urgency for people to be redeemed, we lose the value of the cross. This is unmistakably a part of the character of Christ

The world is not the world it was 12 months ago, regardless of when you are reading this book. We cannot "do" Church like we did last year. There has to be a new urgency to our faith. The world has changed and we need to expand in capacity accordingly or we will become irrelevant. The season we live in DEMANDS that we redefine our understanding of Kingdom and Church. The world that introduced me to missions 40 years ago does not exist anymore.

- We have seen the fall of a communist system that declared "there is no God" and the rise of an Islamic movement declaring "there is only one god"
- We have seen a dramatic shift in the centre of gravity of Christianity with a decline of faith in the "Christian West" and an increase in faith in the "Unreached East"
- We have witnessed, the first time by this generation, the establishment of an Islamic Caliphate. And by the way, if you don't know what this means you are in desperate need of capacity growth
- We currently see the greatest movement of uprooted people in human history . There are more than 67 million uprooted people and refugees in the world today. A harvest field that no generation has witnessed before
- We see more nations involved in warfare than ever before in history — 68 countries and 746 groups. Never before has there been such a need for peace and peacemakers
- In Iraq alone there has been an average of 3 suicide bomb attacks every week for the past 7 years killing an average of 33 people per week

- We see the greatest mission movement in the history of the Church gaining momentum in China – a vision of 200,000 missionaries to be sent along the One Belt One Road initiative of Xi Xingpin, reaching the unreached with the Gospel of Christ. Once again, if this is the first time you hear about this movement there is some serious work ahead of you
- We find today more Muslims coming to know Christ than ever before in history. In Egypt the conservative guesstimate is 4 million converts, in Iran 2 million and in Europe tens of thousands
- We find the tide of secular Europe slowly turning and a possible re-Christianisation of Europe because of the refugees
- In technology we live in amazing times: The world has 2.4 billion Internet users — 34% of the world population – and 6 billion mobile phone users
- Google now processes over 40,000 search queries every second on average, which translates to over 3.5 billion searches a day and 1.2 trillion searches a year worldwide. Every query has to travel on average 1,500 miles to a data centre and back to return the answer to the user. A single Google query uses 1,000 computers in 0.2 seconds to retrieve an answer

Just like Jesus, we must develop a clear sense of our mission in the context of the season we find ourselves in so that we can invest our time wisely with God's calling in mind. There are many good things we can do, but the good can become the enemy of the best, unless we focus intentionally on addressing the priorities and urgencies of our time.

The greatest threat to expanding our behavioural capacity is the busyness of non-essentials that absorbs our attention and time. We live in a future-oriented culture that relates time largely to efficiency and productivity instead of urgency and priority.

In the series CONFORMED TO HIS IMAGE[112] the author explores the reality that the civil religion of the Western World worships the god of progress and inspires us to compete, achieve, and win for the sake of competing, achieving, and winning. Life for many has been colourfully described as a matter of "blowing & going, plotting & planning, ducking & diving, running & gunning, slamming & jamming, moving & shaking, shoving & jiving".

Longshoreman philosopher Eric Hoffer wrote, *"We are warned not to waste time, but we are brought up to waste our lives."* This is evident in the tragedy of many people who in the first half of their lives spend their health looking for wealth, and in the last half spend their wealth looking for health.

We often miss out on the unique opportunities presented to us because we are dominated by excessive Christian activities that do not reflect the urgency of our times. Gordon Dahl put it, *"Most middle-class Americans tend to worship their work, to work at their play, and to play at their worship."*

Meeting with a pastor from Lebanon recently challenged my behavioural capacity and deeply ministered to my heart. Brother Magdi serves to the point of exhaustion among the more than 1.5 million refugees in Lebanon. He said the following: *"The rhythm in heaven has changed. A few years ago converts were trickling into the Kingdom. Now they run to the Lord. The beat in heaven is much faster today. We need to run with heaven."*
We need to run with heaven. But expanding our behavioural capacity will not only come by understanding the urgency, it will need a keen mind to look beyond obligation to opportunity.

FROM OBLIGATION TO OPPORTUNITY

Winston Churchill once said that *"We will never reach our destination if we stop and throw stones at every dog that barks."* Think about Matthew's

---

[112] https://bible.org/seriespage/2-process-spirituality-being-versus-doing

account of one of the greatest sermons ever preached[113]. Jesus preaches to a crowd that gathered on the side of a mountain overlooking the Sea of Galilee, a crowd that consisted of Jewish peasants, farmers, theologians and, most of all, nationalistic Roman-haters. Quite the crowd. In the establishment of a ministry this would normally be the place to say the right things to draw the right crowd. Not Jesus. Suddenly, out of the blue, comes this teaching: *"If anyone forces you to go one mile, go with them two miles. Give to the one who asks you, and do not turn away from the one who wants to borrow from you."*

What a shocker. Not just a "what-an-inspiring-sermon" shocker but a completely "what-the-heck-was-he-thinking" shocker.

Jesus here makes reference to the Roman powers that occupied Israel during this time. Theologically they were seen as gentile, morally they were seen as pagan, nationally they were unwanted, culturally they were foreign and generally they were despised. Herod, who was appointed by Caesar as a puppet king, was known for his murderous acts that even included members of his own family who he believed were plotting to overthrow him. Jewish nationalism was at an all-time high and there must have been more than just a murmur in the crowd.

It was in this context that Jesus said, essentially, *"...if a man asks you to walk a mile with him, do it. Then walk another mile with him."*

Outrageous! Unthinkable! Jesus was clearly referring to the Roman law that permitted any Roman soldier to stop a Jewish man on the road and force him to drop what he was carrying in order to assist the Roman soldier in bearing his load. Or, the solider could have simply made the Jew carry his load out of laziness or a power trip. But the law only required the Israelite

---

[113] Matthew 5:38-42 You have heard that it was said, 'Eye for eye, and tooth for tooth.' But I tell you, do not resist an evil person. If anyone slaps you on the right cheek, turn to them the other cheek also. And if anyone wants to sue you and take your shirt, hand over your coat as well. If anyone forces you to go one mile, go with them two miles. Give to the one who asks you, and do not turn away from the one who wants to borrow from you.

to walk one mile for the soldier. Not two. Only one. Many Jews even marked a mile in all directions from their home and would go not a step further. So Jesus tells His audience to go beyond obligation. The second mile is not an obligation, it is an opportunity. This is the key phrase in expanding our behavioural capacity. We need to establish a vision to look beyond **obligation** and see the **opportunity**.

In an age of fast-food, fast-internet and fast-relations we have cultivated a generation of individuals who quit too quickly and who seek to get by with the absolute minimum. It has become easy to quit after an obligation is completed. In looking for the easiest path we have failed to develop a generation with muscle and the endurance for the second mile. We miss the opportunity that most often lies in doing the difficult and denying our rights to rest, relaxation and respite.

Clayton King, on his blog *"Going the Extra Mile[114]"*, elaborates as follows on this Scripture:

The point in demanding that the Jews walk two miles was for them to show the Romans that they were different from them. They did not demand, they offered. They did not compel, they invited. The children of Israel were operating from a different worldview, one of simplicity and goodness and virtue found in the God of scripture. The Romans operated from a worldview of power, conquest, and greed. Roman hearts could be won, one at a time, by simple acts of radical service that went contrary to the expectation. Freedom was to come not from a Jewish uprising or a revolt, but from the internal liberty of being free to serve your enemy, testifying to the transforming power of God in a person's soul.

The only way for the good to win over the evil was to go beyond the expectation. The second mile in our lives makes the "Roman" world ask why we would go the extra distance under such a heavy burden. The second mile opens up conversations that would never happen in the first mile. The second mile makes us better humans and better Christians. It builds the

---

[114] http://www.claytonking.com/blog/2013/9/2/going-the-extra-mile

muscle we need to carry the gospel and the endurance we need to remain faithful through the seasons of life and not just for a season of life.
Go beyond obligation. You will only find opportunity when you walk the second mile. And don't worry about the burden wearing you out. You can rest when you reach your destination.

The glorious truth is that once we move beyond obligation into the unexpected, we have the opportunity to change lives. Asked by the BBC to identify the defining moment in his life, Desmond Tutu spoke of the day he and his mother were walking down the street. Tutu was nine years old. A tall white man dressed in a black suit came towards them. In the days of apartheid in South Africa, when a black person and a white person met while walking on a footpath, the black person was expected to step off the sidewalk to allow the white person to pass and nod their head as a gesture of respect. But this day, before a young Tutu and his mother could step off the sidewalk the white man stepped off the sidewalk and, as they passed, he tipped his hat in a gesture of respect to her!

The white man was Trevor Huddleston, an Anglican priest who was bitterly opposed to apartheid. It changed Tutu's life. When his mother told him that Trevor Huddleston had stepped off the sidewalk because he was a "man of God," Tutu found his calling. *"When she told me that he was an Anglican priest I decided there and then that I wanted to be an Anglican priest too. And what is more, I wanted to be a man of God"* said Tutu.

Huddleston later became a mentor to Desmond Tutu and his commitment to the equality of all human beings due to their creation in God's image a key driver in Tutu's opposition to apartheid."

My prayer is that we can all strive to be "people of God" who are willing to "step off the sidewalk" and "tip our hat" to our sisters and brothers, particularly those on the margins. May it be so...

Amazingly, once we start building our behavioural capacity we will soon discover the need to build our stamina capacity.

CHAPTER 12
Stamina Capacity
We need to tighten our grip

"Step one to running a marathon: You run. There is no step two."
Barney Stinson on How I met your mother

The key question to answer as we approach the final chapter of the book is **HOW** to build capacity in order to respond to the challenges and opportunities in this season of harvest. The answer is simple; there has to be an increase in our **CAPACITY TO ENDURE** if we want to grow and mature as believers. We must build a ministry toughness if we hope to become agents of change. This will however not be obtained at Bible schools or during Sunday morning services. An increase in stamina, endurance and perseverance can only be "caught", and cannot be "taught".

Most modern-day heroes are remembered for what they achieved instead of being acknowledged for what they overcame. Let's list a few names, from politicians, entrepreneurs, sportsmen and women, actors, musicians and scientists, to understand that greatness lies not in achieving but in overcoming:

- **Pele** — One of the greatest soccer player of all time, was born in conditions of extreme poverty in Sao Paulo. The crime-ridden neighbourhood's despair and hardships allowed Pele to grow a rugged inner force that gave him a strong edge over his competition. He said the following: *"Success is no accident. It is hard work, perseverance, learning, studying, sacrifice and most of all, love of what you are doing or learning to do."*

- **Lionel Messi** — One of the greatest soccer players in modern-history, was diagnosed with growth hormone deficiency at the age of 11. Rather than discourage him, Messi used it to motivate him. He never once grew a "poor me" attitude and he absolutely NEVER made an excuse or complained. Today, Lionel Messi is an ambassador for UNICEF and he created his own charity foundation for struggling children

- **Albert Einstein** — One of the greatest scientists in history, didn't speak until he was four years old. Einstein didn't have the best childhood. In fact, throughout elementary school, many of his teachers thought he was lazy and wouldn't make anything of himself.

- **Jim Carrey** — one of the best comedic actors of an era, used to be homeless and when he was 15, he had to drop out of school to support his family. His father was an unemployed musician and as the family went from "lower middle class to poor", they eventually had to start living in a van. Carrey didn't let this stop him from achieving his dream of becoming a comedian.

- **Benjamin Franklin** — one of America's Founding Fathers dropped out of school at age ten. Franklin's parents could only afford to keep him in school until his tenth birthday. That didn't stop the great man from pursuing his education. He taught himself through voracious reading, and eventually went on to invent the lightning rod and bifocals.

- **Richard Branson** — one of the worlds' most successful entrepreneurs has dyslexia. Branson was a pretty bad student — he didn't get good marks and he did poorly on standardized tests. Instead of giving up, he used the power of his personality to drive him to success. Today, Branson, known for developing Virgin Records and many of its more technologically advanced spinoffs, is the fourth richest person in the UK.

- **Stephen King** — One of the world's leading authors, his first novel was rejected 30 times. If it weren't for King's wife, "Carrie" may not have ever existed. After being consistently rejected by publishing houses, King gave up and threw his first book in the trash. His wife, Tabitha, retrieved the manuscript and urged King to finish it. Now, King's books have sold over 350 million copies and have been made into countless major motion pictures.

- **Oprah Winfrey** — One of the world's leading TV presenters gave birth at age 14 and lost her child. She grew up in Milwaukee, Wis. and was repeatedly molested by her cousin, uncle and a family friend. She eventually ran away from home, and at age 14 gave birth to a baby boy who died shortly after. But Winfrey's tragic past didn't stop her from becoming the force she is today. She excelled as an honours student in high school, and won an oratory contest which secured her a full scholarship to college. Now the entrepreneur and personality has the admiration of millions and a net worth of $2.9 billion.

- **Thomas Edison** — One of the greatest inventors in history failed 1,000 times before creating the lightbulb. Although the exact number of tries has been debated, ranging from 1,000 to 10,000 attempts, it's safe to say Edison tried and failed a whole lot before he successfully created his beacon of light. His response to his repeated failures? "I have not failed. I've just found 10,000 ways that won't work."

- **Vincent Van Gogh** — One of the greatest artists of all time only sold one painting in his lifetime. Even though he made no money, he still painted over 900 works of art. Though his persistence went unnoticed when he was alive, Van Gogh proves you don't need external validation to be proud of the work you create.

- **Franklin Roosevelt** — One of the greatest politicians in US history, became partially paralyzed at 39. After vacationing in Canada, Roosevelt developed polio, which eventually left him paralyzed from the waist down for the rest of his life. Even though he couldn't walk, he went on to lead the country as one of the most respected and memorable presidents in history.

- **Simon Cowell** — One of the biggest forces in reality television had a failed record company. By his late twenties, Cowell had made a million dollars and lost a million dollars. Cowell told The Daily Mail in 2012, *"'I've had many failures. The biggest was when my record company went bust."* Even after such a momentous loss, Cowell picked himself up and began serving as a judge for "Pop Idol", "The X Factor", "Britain's Got Talent" and "American Idol". Forbes has estimated his net worth at $95 million.

- **Charlize Theron** — One of the most successful South African actresses of all time, witnessed her mother kill her father. When Theron was 15, she witnessed her mother shoot her alcoholic father in an act of self defence. Instead of letting the trauma immobilize her ambition, Theron channelled her energy into making a name for herself. She would eventually become one of the most respected and talented actresses, becoming the first South African actress to win an Academy Award.

- **Steven Spielberg** — One of the most prolific filmmakers of all time, the man who brought us "Shindler's List", "Jaws", "E.T." and "Jurassic Park" couldn't get into the film school of his choice. In the end, Spielberg would get the last laugh, when USC awarded him an honorary degree in 1994. Two years later, he became a trustee of the university that rejected him.

- **Michael Jordan** — One of the best basketball players of all time was actually cut from his high school basketball team. Luckily, Jordan didn't let this setback stop him from playing the game, and as he once stated in a famous ad, "I have missed more than 9,000 shots in my career. I have lost almost 300 games. On 26 occasions I have been entrusted to take the game-winning shot, and I missed. I have failed over and over and over again in my life. And that is why I succeed."

- **Fred Astaire** — One of the most successful actors/singers/dancers of his era was told in his first screen test by the testing director of MGM that he "Can't act. Can't sing. Slightly bald. Not handsome. Can dance a little." Astaire went on to become an incredibly successful actor/singer/dancer and kept that note in his Beverly Hills home to remind him of where he came from.

Building our capacity in endurance and building spiritual stamina will involve three principles:
- From pruning — to prosperous
- From victim — to victorious
- From haste — to heart

FROM PRUNING — TO PROSPEROUS

Before looking at the **HOW** of building stamina, we need to look at the **WHEN** of building stamina.

One of the main obstacles to capacity building is the fact that we often seek favourable "seasons" to build capacity. We attend conference after conference with an admirable desire to get to know God more and to understand Scripture more deeply, but often lack the stamina to apply those lessons when "life happens". We love hearing about the persecuted Church and are inspired by testimonies of those who gave all for the glory of God, and yet we protect our freedom and rights with equal religious zeal. These are all important components in growing as believers but also present the risk of becoming obese believers with lots of nutrition but little stamina.

In John 15:2[115] the Lord teaches His disciples a contradistinctive lesson in capacity building. This hard lesson explains the principle that the worst of

---

[115] John 15:2 He cuts off every branch in me that bears no fruit, while every branch that does bear fruit he prunes so that it will be even more fruitful.

times are very often the best of times. The promise Jesus made to His followers, is that further growth is the blessed reward of forward growth and that to ensure capacity we will need pruning, pain and purpose, not safety, security and sanctuary.

I remember walking through a vineyard with a wine farmer just after the grapes were harvested when he took his secateurs and started describing the process and the need for pruning. *"Pruning is not only to get rid of dead branches and a cleaning process, it is to stimulate and initiate new growth,"* he said. *"New growth occurs right where you make the cut. The more buds that are pruned, the greater the capacity for new growth."* He then referred to John 15 and explained that a fruitful harvest is completely dependent on the painful process of pruning. It is about growth, capacity and stamina. It is about stimulating vision for future harvests.

Make no mistake, pruning is painful. And even though we as Christians do not pursue hardships and pain, we can never shy away from it or ignore it. This is where capacity is impregnated.

The irony is that where most religions see hardship as a curse or a result of sin, Christians see it an act of love and a discipline to grow[116]. Hardship is a time where Christ invests His care into those He loves by stimulating growth and building endurance. We should never ignore the seasons of pruning, although it will involve pain and happen in our spiritual seasons of winter.

I vividly remember meeting brother Ibrahim, an Egyptian believer who was arrested in Libya for distributing Bibles. He shared how he was imprisoned and tortured for days without end. Ibrahim cried out to the Lord in his distress and pleaded with the Lord to stop the suffering and to release him from prison. *"Then the Lord spoke to me,"* said Ibrahim with a smile. *"And what He said to me took me by surprise. 'Stop being a baby!' the Lord said to me. 'When you volunteered to be in ministry did you not deny yourself, die to yourself and become committed to the cross as I was? Did you not*

---

[116] Revelation 3:19 Those whom I love I rebuke and discipline. So be earnest and repent.

embrace a life of sacrifice and self-denial? Now stop crying like a baby and act like a man!'"

Ibrahim was later released but we sensed when he spoke that the time in prison was a time of pruning that resulted in building a greater capacity in his life than all the years in freedom put together.

So, understanding the WHEN of stamina building helps us to pursue the HOW of stamina building.

FROM VICTIM — TO VICTORIOUS

It never ceases to amaze me how often well-meant words of encouragement, even prophesies that so often limit capacity building and hinder endurance, are spoken to people in need. We seem to proclaim release more than endurance. When friends are sick it is so easy to speak prophesies of healing instead of words of perseverance. When times are tough it takes little effort to speak promises of release, instead of encouraging endurance. Capacity building will never come in times of comfort and every challenge should be seen as divine moments of growth, and should be advocated as such by friends and family.

Theodore Roosevelt once said the following:
"It is not the critic who counts; not the man who points out how the strong man stumbles, or where the doer of deeds could have done them better. The credit belongs to the man who is actually in the arena, whose face is marred by dust and sweat and blood; who strives valiantly; who errs, who comes short again and again, because there is no effort without error and shortcoming; but who does actually strive to do the deeds; who knows great enthusiasms, the great devotions; who spends himself in a worthy cause; who at the best knows in the end the triumph of high achievement, and who at the worst, if he fails, at least fails while daring greatly, so that his place shall never be with those cold and timid souls who neither know victory nor defeat."

"...those cold and timid souls who neither know victory nor defeat." These are challenging words for those who seek to practise a safe and risk-free religion. I remember meeting a Christian in a restricted country and as we departed he asked if he could pray for me. I always value the prayers of those who carry the cross and eagerly accepted the blessing. The brother prayed and then ended with these short and uncomfortable words: *"May the Lord deny you peace and grant you victory."*

As I opened my eyes and he saw the questions in my eyes, he responded as follows: *"My brother, how will you ever experience victory if you only live in peace."*

Our mandate as believers is to live lives that will reflect a victory rooted in the inner peace of the cross that Christ secured, not in the comforts of the peace that the world offers. That was the reason why Jesus looked at His disciples and rebuked Peter in the harshest possible way. "Get behind me, Satan!" he said. "You do not have in mind the concerns of God, but merely human concerns." (Mark 8:33)

The ability to persevere in times of hardship will ironically both *require* endurance and at the same time also *build* endurance. It is the contradistinctive nature of trials that they not only build character, but also reveal character. The ability to endure in difficult times does not only depend on how we deal with hardships at the time but on how we dealt with them in the past. Every hardship therefore becomes a conduit to build a new capacity of endurance for future hardships.

The apostle Paul is an excellent example of this. After his dramatic encounter with Christ on the road to Damascus, the first lesson he had to learn was to build a capacity for future endurance. The Lord told Ananias that *"I will show him how much he must suffer for My name"* (Acts 9:16). Not *"I will show him how powerfully he will witness for My name"* or *"how successful he will be in ministry"* but simply *"how much he will suffer for My name"*. This was the first step in Paul's process of building a capacity for what he would endure in the future. This provided the building blocks as preparation for surviving imprisonments, floggings, beatings, stonings, shipwrecks, hunger and various other trials (2 Corinthians 11:23-26). Paul had the stamina to endure the fiercest opposition because his capacity to endure was not based on false promises of release but an ever evolving confrontation with hardships.

Like Paul we need to tighten our grip when going through hardships and use every trial as an opportunity to expand our capacity for endurance.

FROM HASTE — TO HEART

Grant Lovejoy[117] compares the approach of some Christians to ministry to that of a Cheetah. He writes as follows:

A recent television documentary pointed out that the cheetah survives on the African plains by running down its prey. The big cat can sprint seventy miles per hour. But the cheetah cannot sustain that pace for long. Within its long, sleek body is a disproportionately small heart, which causes the cheetah to tire quickly. Unless the cheetah catches its prey in the first flurry, it must abandon the chase. Sometimes Christians seem to have the cheetah's approach to ministry. We speed into projects with great energy. But lacking the heart for sustained effort, we fizzle before we finish. We vow to start faster and run harder, when what we need may be not more speed but more staying power--stamina that comes only from a bigger heart. Motion and busyness, no matter how great, yield nothing unless we allow God to give us the heart.

As post-modern Christians we all have evolved from the early days of normal-Christian-martyrdom to live an inevitable "double-life" where we still believe in the theology of sacrifice but do everything in our power to avoid it. Within the safe walls of our religion, we often "faint" at the thought of losing our freedom and our rights to worship. We try to escape the harsh realities of the "outside" world and this often manifests itself in

---

[117] http://www.sermonillustrations.com/a-z/s/stamina.htm

newfound theologies that promote a Gospel of wealth, health and prosperity rather than a Gospel of substance and stamina. Modern-day believers have become masters in finding Scriptures that justify a sacrifice-free lifestyle. Or even worse, we have become masters in applying Scriptures of persecution to our own circumstances of comfort to somehow justify a lifestyle of ease and abundance and still feel connected to Scripture.

It has become a dangerous trend in Western theology that everything is measured relative to our own circumstances. There is the growing view that while Christians are persecuted elsewhere, we suffer in the West too. Some suggest it can be more difficult to be a faithful Christian in the developed world with all its freedoms and wealth than in a poor country with persecution.

To argue that materialism and wealth somehow make it more difficult to follow Christ than living in grinding poverty is deeply problematic both theologically and ethically. *It dismisses or diminishes the actual sufferings of our fellow believers and turns us into victims.* This results in apathy towards the suffering of the global Church and encourages us to be insular and self-obsessed. It is empirically wrong, (no, following Christ is not normally difficult here in the West) and ethically corrupt (they, not we, are being victimised and we are the ones in a position to help).

These theologies of relativism lull us into a sense of comfort and, together with a life-style that so easily conforms to the patterns of the world, create a toxic combination of spiritual obesity and a lack of stamina.

James Emery White gives a personal exhortation on his blog Church and Culture[118]:
"When I was a boy, I was given a piece of paper that moulded my thinking. I had it on my bedroom wall for years until it finally just fell apart with age. It was the words of Calvin Coolidge, 30th President of the United States, that

---

[118] http://www.churchandculture.org/

he delivered in a speech on January 17, 1925. It was titled, "Press On." He said: 'Nothing in the world can take the place of perseverance. Talent will not; nothing is more common than unsuccessful men with talent. Genius will not; unrewarded genius is almost a proverb. Education will not; the world is full of educated derelicts. Persistence and determination alone are omnipotent.

"What marks the life of someone who lives a consequential life for Christ? When you read the lives of the great men and women in the Bible, what marked their lives? Courage? No, they were often afraid. The absence of failure? No, they made more than their fair share of mistakes and many were repeated moral failures.

"What marked their lives was an internal drive that was based on one thing: a hunger for God and the things of God. A desire to forget what is behind and strain toward what is ahead. They were marked by persistence and determination. ... but up."

Perhaps the best description in Scripture to "press on" and "to take heart" is found in **Galatians** 6:9[119] where we are encouraged to "faint not".

"Faint not" requires stamina and spiritual toughness, two traits that come through exercise and determination.

Here is a list of EIGHT certainties in life, things we can expect to face in one form or another, and how we can use them as capacity builders for stamina.

Faint not in times of silence. *LISTEN*
Psalm 46:10 He says, "Be still, and know that I am God."

It is in the times of revelation that we need to obey and the times of silence that we need to listen. We often live within a spiritual paradox that views

---

[119] Galatians 6:9-10 KJV And let us not be weary in well doing: for in due season we shall reap, if we faint not.

times of silence as times of being abandoned instead of times of intimacy. Loneliness refers to a state in which you are unhappy about being alone. Solitude, however, is an aloneness in which you find strength. Christ often pursued solitude in order to spend time with the Father *(John 16:32 "A time is coming... when you will leave Me all alone. Yet I am not alone, for My Father is with Me")*. By using His times of solitude wisely, Jesus was able to use the times of isolation as opportunities to prepare Himself for the cross ahead.

Faint not in times of lack. *TRUST*
Psalm 31:14 But I trust in you, LORD; I say, "You are my God."

One of the silent predicaments of our present time is for Christians to discern between faith and trust. These two virtues are often confused: many who proclaim a FAITH in an omnipotent, spectacular God do not TRUST in His involvement or abilities, setting Him aside as an impotent, spectator God. On the journey of faith we should not only express the belief that God is sovereign, we should act like He is still in control of our lives, our nations, our finances and our families. FAITH is believing in God. TRUST is believing the God we believe in.

Faint not in times of abundance. *SHARE*
2 Corinthians 8:13 "Our desire is not that others might be relieved while you are hard pressed, but that there might be equality."

Abundance can be as incapacitating as poverty if approached incorrectly. If you are blessed with more than your immediate need – share! According to Scripture, God's economic guidelines promote neither wealth nor poverty. The Bible promotes:
- *CONTENTMENT (Hebrews 13:5 "Keep your lives free from the love of money and be content"),*
- *GENEROSITY (2 Corinthians 9:11 "You will be enriched in every way so that you can be generous on every occasion")*

- and *EQUALITY (2 Corinthians 8:13 "Our desire is not that others might be relieved while you are hard pressed, but that there might be equality")*.

These are the three pillars of abundance that should be our guidelines in building capacity.

Faint not in times of waiting. *ENDURE*
Psalm 37:7 Be still before the LORD and wait patiently for Him.

A popular tongue-in-cheek poster reads as follows: "Patience is such a waste of time." At first, this statement seems to contradict James' instruction to be patient and to stand firm. But, as with most things in life, our perceptions are mostly determined by our definitions. If we define patience as "waiting", it is indeed a waste of time. But when patience is understood in a true Biblical context, as "the position of endurance under difficult circumstances", it becomes the sustaining force enabling perseverance in the face of delay. The journey of faith will require this virtue in large quantities and at frequent intervals.

Faint not in times of disappointment: *REMEMBER*
Psalm 77:11 I will remember the deeds of the LORD;

No matter how many challenges we face: **Remember Jesus.** Call to remembrance the faithfulness of the Lord. The fact that you can read this means you still have eyes to see, a brain to comprehend, a voice to pray and a heart to love. Psalm 77 is clearly divided into two parts; Depression and Victory, and the only action that divides the two is the action of verse 11 *"But I will remember..."* David speaks very specifically of how his soul refused to be comforted and how he fell into a pit of despair, depression and hopelessness. But then comes a clear change in his spirit when he chooses to remember — he makes an intentional decision, he says, "But I will remember". Make your life a life of choosing to remember. Choose to remember the goodness of a Saviour.

Faint not in times of failure: *RISE*

Proverbs 24:16 for though the righteous fall seven times, they rise again, but the wicked stumble when calamity strikes.

One of the biggest challenges we all face is the challenge of "**image maintenance**". We all work extremely hard to maintain the perceptions other people have of us – we do this more than working on who we really are. Once the perception of who we are is dented, we experience failure. The response is therefore to find our identity in Christ, how He sees us and how we find our righteousness in Him, not in success or failure as determined by others. We *will* make mistakes in life. This is a given! Faint not in times of failure. This we know — Rise! Not because we are perfect but because we are in Christ.

Faint not in times of sadness: *HOPE*

Psalm 39:7 "But now, Lord, what do I look for? My hope is in you."

No matter what life might throw at us, we all have this blessed assurance that, even though we might be depressed, saddened, disappointed, rejected and isolated by man, we will never be abandoned by God. Nothing, not *"trouble or hardship or persecution or famine or nakedness or danger or sword can separate us from a loving God... nothing in all creation will be able to separate us from the love of God that is already found in Christ Jesus our Lord" (Romans 8:35-39).* This is a powerful Scripture to remember in times of sadness – it is not the promise of a fallible human being, but the words of One who has proven His faithfulness by dying on the cross. Jesus is loyal in times of loneliness not because He said so, but because He proved so. This allows us to have hope in our times of sadness: hope in the knowledge that nothing will separate us from the love of God, and hope in the promise that Jesus will always be with us, to the "very end of the age" (Matthew 28:19).

Faint not in times of victory: *STAY HUMBLE*

James 4:6 But he gives us more grace. That is why Scripture says: "God opposes the proud but shows favor to the humble."

A big challenge in life is not to remain faithful in our times of defeat but to remain humble in our times of victory. Nowhere in Scripture do we read that the Lord despises those who fail, scorns those who makes mistakes, or abandons those who doubt. But we do read that the Lord opposes the proud. Be careful how you receive, acknowledge and report your success. Give God the glory, always.

CONCLUSION
Capacity building
Fifteen stories of capacity growth

Allow me to conclude this journey with an important reminder. Building capacity as a Christian is **NOT** our ultimate goal. It is simply a means of growing into our ultimate goal which is receiving, absorbing, containing and imparting the fullness of Christ. The larger our capacity to be intimate with Christ, the more we have the ability to reflect Christ and influence society. However, confusing the means of obtaining our spiritual goals with the goals themselves could be disastrous.

In an adaptation of Richard Rohr's *"ARE YOU EAGER TO LOVE"*, we find the following comforting advice:
"Mutual presence or intimacy is the ultimate goal of the spiritual journey. Perhaps this is why images of bride and bridegroom are so commonly used by the prophets, the Song of Songs, John the Baptist, Jesus, and in the last verses of the Bible where the marriage is symbolically consummated (Revelation 19:7; 21:2, 9; 22:17).

"Remember, presence does not happen in the mind. All the mind can handle is before and after; it does not know how to be present in the now. That is the mind's great limitation. For this reason you don't have to figure it all out or get everything right ahead of time. You just have to stay on the full journey. None of us know how to be perfect, but we can practice staying in union, staying connected. "Remain in me and I remain in you," says Jesus (see John 15:7[120]). It is about abiding, not performing. It is about holding to

---

[120] John 15:4 (KJV) Abide in me, and I in you. As the branch cannot bear fruit of itself, except it abide in the vine; no more can ye, except ye abide in me. I am the vine, ye are the branches: He that abideth in me, and I in him, the same bringeth forth much fruit: for without me ye can do nothing. If a man abide not in me, he is cast forth as a branch, and is withered; and men gather them, and cast them into the fire, and they are burned. If ye abide in me, and my words abide in you, ye shall ask what ye

your core identity more than perfect behaviour—which would only make you proud and self-sufficient—even if it were possible.

"Every day and in every way, we must choose to live in love. It is mostly a decision, not a feeling. We must even be eager to learn the ever-deeper ways of love (creating capacity) which follow from every decision to love."

So, what can be more appropriate than to conclude this book by learning from those who have kept their intimacy with God through brokenness, persecution and obedience.

Through nearly 40 years of ministry I have been blessed and humbled to meet the proverbial "clouds of witnesses" that Hebrews 12[121] so gloriously refers to. Those who have "thrown off everything" and have "run with perseverance the race marked out for them". Those that "fixed their eyes on Jesus, the pioneer and perfector of their faith and who have endured their own crosses" in expanding their capacity for a season of harvest and such a time as this.

I have had the indescribable joy to sit at their feet and learn. They became friends, soulmates and mentors in my life and challenged me to continuously be transformed by the renewal of my mind. Through listening to their stories, watching their lives and observing their obedience my "spiritual capacity", my growth, my maturity, my reach, my influence and ultimately my capability to transform into the image of Christ were challenged to the core.

---

will, and it shall be done unto you. Herein is my Father glorified, that ye bear much fruit; so shall ye be my disciples.

[121] Hebrews 12:1-2 Therefore, since we are surrounded by such a great cloud of witnesses, let us throw off everything that hinders and the sin that so easily entangles. And let us run with perseverance the race marked out for us, fixing our eyes on Jesus, the pioneer and perfecter of faith. For the joy set before him he endured the cross, scorning its shame, and sat down at the right hand of the throne of God.

I have asked them to share their thoughts on how they built capacity in different areas of their lives. These are the stories, and the lessons of those who have exercised their faith and expanded their capacity in the following:

- ALTITUDE – our elevation
- AMPLITUDE – our fullness
- APTITUDE – our ability
- ATTITUDE – our approach
- CERTITUDE – our conviction
- EXACTITUDE – our precision
- FORTITUDE – our courage
- LATITUDE – our flexibility
- QUIETUDE – our calmness
- RECTITUDE – our righteousness
- SERVITUDE – our servanthood
- SOLICITUDE – our attentiveness

ALTITUDE – our elevation

This exercise develops our capacity to monitor our position, our standing and our elevation before God.

*Psalm 145:14 The LORD **up**holds all who fall and **lifts up** all who are **bowed down**.*

DR. DANIEL SHAYESTEH, a former radical Islamic leader and teacher of Islam in the militant Free Islamic Revolutionary Movement of Iran, was closely associated with the Ayatollah Khomeini in his ultimate rise to power. Daniel was also one of the founder members of Hezbollah in Iran. However, after falling out of favour with Khomeini's political group, he escaped to Turkey where there began an amazing journey to faith in Jesus Christ. Daniel understood the challenge of rebuilding his capacity in his new position before God.

Daniel shares as follows:
I have come from an Islamic family in Iran. Since childhood, I learned popular lessons such as "truth is secondary to harmony" or, "criticism could end up exposing your family to an unending deprivation, discrimination or attack", or, "be aware that there are mice in the house; they can spread the news." Imagine the effects of these fearful lessons in blocking your ability to lead a creative life in your society.

In 1979, the paralyzing fear broke as the Shah left Iran and the country fell into the hands of we revolutionaries under the leadership of Ayatollah Khomeini. I was initially invited to ignite the start of the Hezbollah (the Revolutionary Army) in Iran for protecting and exporting the Revolution. Soon after, through a religious game, a resolution was passed in the parliament which gave absolute authority to Khomeini allowing him to have unquestionable right over everything and everyone, including the president elect. This was totally against the promise of Khomeini before the revolution. I protested, got a death sentence, but was able to escape to Turkey where there was still a bit of freedom.

In Turkey I enrolled in a doctorate course, majoring in How Cultures, Religions and Ideas Shape Attitudes, including leadership. I discovered that in Christianity a Christian had not only a right to reason with leaders but with his (her) God too (Isaiah 1:18), since God desired people to get their ability into work for advancing in everything good and creative.

This seemed to me like rising from the death of restriction to such a freedom which releases your conscience to stretch your capacity for learning to cross barriers, grow and become a vessel of growth too. Soon after, Jesus won my heart by giving solid reasons about everything in life so that I could overcome my own selfish character, inherited social obstacles and walk with Him into others' lives by manifesting the changes in myself as examples of His work.

He inspired me to practically prove that I was born again in His limitless image and therefore had the capacity to make Him known as my BELOVED ONE to everyone since the true love necessitates 100% commitment and does not remain quiet, no matter what the cost may be.

- Daniel is the President of **Exodus From Darkness**, a specialized apologetics and evangelistic ministry for revealing the values of Christ in every part of life so that people can put their trust in Him with confidence. Contact Daniel for teaching and speaking: 7spirits@gmail.com or www.exodusfromdarkness.org.

AMPLITUDE – our fullness

This exercise develops our capacity in fullness and wholeness and to keep on filling up. Remember, unless our input exceeds our output, our upkeep will be our downfall.

*Acts 2:28 You have made known to me the paths of life; you will **fill me** with joy in your presence.*

MARK ZHOU is the Director of Bridges International Consultants, a business-as-mission leadership training network based in Hong Kong, for the purpose of mobilizing and equipping marketplace leaders to fulfil the Great Commission through their business platforms.

Mark shares as follows:
Though having moved our home back to Asia for the last 13 years, I still constantly travel between China and overseas, therefore this kind of sojourner's life style keeps me from settling down as a real "permanent resident" of Hong Kong. On the other hand, it's indeed the Holy Spirit's work I have witnessed in different places that refreshes my soul at the core, so what can I say more on the topic of "Building Capacity in FULLNESS?"

***Praying in the Spirit** on all occasions and **seeking God's perspective** in all situations are on my top list of "capacity builders." Every time when I come to realize that in all things God works for the good of those who love him, who have been called according to his purpose, immediately there is an increase in my spiritual capacity. Ultimately, it's not the matter of "being well fed or hungry, living in plenty or in want," as Apostle Paul has learned the secret of being content in any and every situation; it is the Lord who gives us strength to do everything and we are more than conquerors through Him who loves us!*

*I also believe that becoming aware of the **spiritual leakage** is equally important. Once the leaking factor has been identified, we also can learn* *from Paul's discipline— "No, I beat my body and make it my slave so that after I have preached to others, I myself will not be disqualified for the prize."—1 Cor. 9:26. In other words, without any mercy on our flesh but with undivided devotion to Jesus, we should be able to take hold of the life that is truly life and position ourselves to embrace the abundant life that Jesus has promised!*

- Contact Mark for teaching and speaking: bridgeshk@gmail.com

APTITUDE – our ability

This exercise expands our capacity by intentionally using our giftings and our talents for Kingdom purposes.

John 15:5 "I am the vine; you are the branches. If you remain in me and I in you, you will bear much fruit; apart from me you can do nothing."

BILL DRAKE knows what it is to feel hurt, rejected and without hope. At the age of 19 he was playing piano in bars and nightclubs in his native America and was on the brink of ending what he describes as his "unlovely life." Only by the grace of God, did he not commit suicide. God radically changed his life and began to use his musical gifting to challenge and encourage many others. Several years later George Verwer, founder of Operation Mobilization, heard Bill lead worship at Biola University in California and threw out a challenge: *"How can you play and sing songs like that if you are not willing to back it up with your lifestyle?"* George went on to challenge Bill to live the commitment he was singing about and join OM as International Music Minister. After graduating from Biola, Bill did this, living in England for 10 years with his wife Teri and their two daughters, Shelby and Sharayah.

Since then, Bill has been privileged to minister in over 50 countries. In 2009 Bill was a Founder and first Director of OM Arts International, the creative arts ministry of Operation Mobilization International. Partnering with other leaders in OM who were engaged in Dance, Drama, Visual Arts, Music, and Ethnodoxology, Bill and team forged a unique ministry within the larger fellowship of OM, actively engaging with local artistic believers in bringing the Gospel of Jesus Christ in many countries in Europe, the Middle East, and around the world.

Most recently Bill has been asked to lead a new Division in OM Internationally, called Catalytic Ministries. This not only includes Arts, but also Sports, Aids, Business as Mission, Teen Ministry, Muslim Diaspora Ministry, Sex Trafficking, and Relief & Development. This promotion opens a Global Ministry to Bill, to engage with Jesus followers all over the world to help them express their faith and worship through their God-given gifts, talents, and expertise.

Bill shares as follows:
Capacity is that quality of a vessel that relates to what it is capable or not capable of receiving, handling, and holding. When it comes to a Kingdom of God understanding, it has aspects of "availability", "scope", and "stewardship" woven into its definition.

There are hints of this all throughout scripture. Concerning Israel: "He came to His own and His own received Him not". Concerning Fruit: The Fig Tree either did not have the capacity to bear fruit, or chose not to. But the topic of Capacity seems to come most to the forefront in scripture when it comes to Jesus' teaching on New Wine, and Wineskins.

This teaching of course instructs us that new things should not be put in reused old structures. As Sarah Groves puts so well in her song, Painting Pictures of Egypt, "The places that used to fit me cannot hold the things I've learned..." obviously once one has experienced new things in the Lord, not only are you never the same, but you can't go back. Old paradigms were not built to hold the goodness and newness that has now been poured in, and both will be irreparably damaged if you try. Revival has always produced new constructs for vibrant communities of Jesus followers – things that refuse to reform need to brace for inevitable irrelevancy...

But this teaching also assumes something that I have recently found absolutely evident in my own life: the preparation of the New Wineskin precedes the arrival of the New Wine! In other words, before God has ever used me or done something through me, He always first prepares me, even if I have not the slightest clue what for! The Lord needs to make "room" first, for more of Himself, His gifting, and His wisdom, and although I might be focused on the excitement of the new thing, I need to be prepared for how He likes to work – He first needs to create more capacity in me – and the process of that is every bit as much important as the new thing He is wanting to pour in.

So many of us have been witness to the damage caused by giving someone who is immature, ignorant, untrained or unprepared, too much responsibility. And while such an experience can at times seem to cause someone to step up and grow, many times it not only damages the person who is then all at once put under too much pressure, but the toxic waste that then spills out of that person proceeds to then infect everyone else around them. More often than not, when it seems like someone unprepared has somehow miraculously been able to take on more than anyone ever thought they should, it is usually found out later that God all along had been increasing their capacity before the "new wine" ever hit them.

So while it is true that everyone who ever had the privilege of being greatly used of God got called into radial, unconditional, obedience, they were also called into a desert, a furnace, a lion's den, a prison, another country, a crucible from which they would emerge totally changed; an enlargement of their capacity, with a new ability to be that much more pliable, that much more adaptable, in order to contain something that much more dynamic, transformative, and ultimately supernatural that produced eternal results.

Do anything, that you have to do to me
so you can do anything, that you want to do through me
Break anything, that you have to break in me
Then release anything that you want to flow through me

Bill Drake – "Sacred Surrender" © 2005 Old Dirt Road Music

- To invite Bill to your Church or group, visit his website at: https://www.billdrake.com/contact

ATTITUDE – our approach

This exercise develops our capacity to approach unexpected challenges with a different mindset and to reposition ourselves mentally when the odds are suddenly stacked against us.

Ephesians 4:23 to be made new in the attitude of your minds.

CURT VAHLE is a part of INcontext USA team. He also is a licensed Insurance Agent specializing in Long-Term Care Insurance and lives in Indianapolis, Indiana with his wife Judy. He is the father of three daughters, a son, and five beautiful grandchildren.

Shortly before an outreach to the Middle East in 2017, Curt was diagnosed with Multiple Myeloma, bone marrow cancer, and life made a sudden unexpected and irreversible turn. The arduous process of healing involved days and weeks of testing, and several rounds of initial chemotherapy each lasting 21 days. Then stem cell collection consisting of IV access with two lines put in near his collarbone, daily injections to stimulate his stem cells, removing his blood from his body through one IV line, filtering through a machine where the stem cells were separated and collected, and then his blood was put back into his body through the other IV lumen. After that, Curt spent days in isolation being subjected to a very heavy-duty chemo medication and having his stem cells transplanted back into his body. He suffered the undesirable side effects that are most common with cancer treatments such as nausea, hair loss, mouth sores, diarrhoea, fatigue, etc.

Keeping faith came naturally for Curt and Judy, and building capacity came joyfully. One hundred days in isolation solidified an attitude in the hearts of Curt and Judy that few believers are willing to learn the easy way.
Curt shares as follows:
*When I think about **"Building Capacity"** and what that means to me, I think about **enlarging my territory, and increasing my effectiveness for God.***

*Every believer has this aspiration. Here in America you can listen to thousands of messages, all seemingly with the answer on how to get from A-Z. Advice is everywhere and quite abundant. One thing not usually mentioned in these messages, is the factor of **preparation through the process of TIME**!*

When I started going after the things of the Lord in 1975, I was as enthusiastic as you could get. I was all about "Building Capacity;" reaching the world, preaching the Gospel, getting into fulltime ministry. Full of zeal but without understanding, that was me. What was missing? Looking back 43 years later, I realize the thing that was missing, and what I wish I'd been told and taught early on was this. If you want to build capacity, it takes time, and slowing down so as not to miss what's right in front of you. I can tell you, I missed a lot. We live in such a fast-paced world, and unfortunately the process of building capacity does not. It takes time and experiential knowledge. I can only speak for myself, and some of these may not apply to you, but here are a few things I've come to realize when it comes to "Building Capacity."

1. *Everything starts with a love for Jesus and a heart for God and his word. Without this, it won't happen.*
2. *God and his grace will supply all your needs and desires, but on **HIS** timeline. This took years to understand. Dave Ramsey says one definition of maturity is learning to delay pleasure. Everybody wants instant growth. Unfortunately, that's a carnival Christianity pipe dream that leads to nowhere.*
3. *Philippians 3:14 I press on toward the goal to win the prize for which God has called me heavenward in Christ Jesus. This is so important! Through thick and thin, keep moving forward. For me, the greatest revelation and understanding on how to connect with the lost, with a right heart, and how to relate to Christ's Body (the Church), came through what you would call bad or negative experiences. That's right, the highlights and greatest growth in my life came through bad or negative experiences!*

4. *Lastly, but extremely important, be yourself! Don't compare yourself with other Christians, this only feeds a religious spirit. The lost will see right through you! To "Build Capacity" you've got to be comfortable in your own skin.*

There is a simplicity in Christ that once realized lifts all burdens and drives away condemnation, and is THE WAY to truly "Build Capacity."

- Curt is currently heading INcontext International in the USA and can be contacted for more information and speaking engagements: curt@incontextministries.org

CERTITUDE – our conviction

This exercise develops our capacity to hold on to our convictions, our certainties and our confidence even when life makes a U-turn and things do not go the way we planned.

Psalm 42:5 Why, my soul, are you downcast? Why so disturbed within me? Put your hope in God, for I will yet praise him, my Savior and my God.

HAKIM is a leader in the Arab World, training Christian entrepreneurs to use their businesses as platforms for sharing the love of Christ. In early April 2007 a group of Arab students were commissioned to various countries in North Africa after a discipleship training school. Hakim led one of the teams that travelled to a remote village where the people were still unreached and untouched by the Gospel of Christ.

The team travelled from village to village where they showed the Jesus film and witnessed about their relationship with Christ. Then, one evening in a matter of seconds, all the teachings and theology the students learnt in the months before, suddenly became a reality. On the evening of April 26 as they were leaving one of the villages they were ambushed by armed gunmen. The driver drove away as quickly as possible, but a number of students on the truck were wounded in the shooting. Four of them died.

While driving in the dark in search of the nearest hospital, Hakim phoned his wife, back at home, with the tragic news of four soul-mates that gave their lives for Christ. But Hakim also had other news to share. He had a new certainty that they, as a family, were to return to this region as full-time witnesses for Christ.

Today Hakim and his family still serve the Lord in the Arab world. There have been evictions, opposition, pain and hardship but their certitude that God has called them has always been the determining factor in pursuing a life of faithfulness.

Hakim shares as follows:

I always thought my faith and my convictions were very strong and stable all the time, but now I think this is one of the biggest mistakes I made in my life! If we look at our faith as an idea or even as an ideology we believe in, it becomes a one-off event and that's it. I'm not sure if this approach would work, even if it can work for some believers. I think we will be missing so much in our life with the Lord.

I see my life with the Lord as a journey and through the years I could see how my faith became stronger. I recognize the times when I couldn't even believe, and yet He did it for me. Through the years I had my good days but I also had my very bad days. Sometimes it was so hard that I was almost sure I couldn't continue, but these were the times when I experienced God the most because I simply had no option but to run to Him.

Every time I had a situation like this there was pain, struggle, lots of pressure and sometimes even doubts, but I always got out of it with a deeper conviction and a bigger capacity in my heart to have the certainty that He is my Father, He is there for me and for sure He is worth it to live for.

I believe giving up should never be an option in our lives as followers of Jesus. Not because we are heroes or because we are so clever by ourselves. If we trust Him enough we cannot allow the world around us to push us to surrender easily when it's hard or painful, or even when it's not according to our plans or if it doesn't go as we like. It all comes back to how deep our trust and our faith is rooted in Him.

Do we really trust Him? Do we really know that He is our Father and He cares for us? Do we really believe in our heart that He is worthy of our life?

EXACTITUDE – our precision

This exercise develops our capacity to witness with greater excellence and precision; to develop a discipline in faithfulness, not only in serving Christ but especially in the ministry that has been entrusted to us, regardless of how big or how small in the eyes of man.

Ephesians 4:1 As a prisoner for the Lord, then, I urge you to live a life worthy of the calling you have received.

GERALD LAUCHE is a German national who has been pastoring and leading a ministry in the Middle East for more than 31 years. He shares a deep passion for the People Groups in the south of Egypt and the north of Sudan together with his wife Ingrid and his five daughters who were all raised in the Middle East. Gerald understands the challenge of surrendering to a foreign culture and adapting a new world-view, following different approaches and acquiring new habits for the sake of Christ.

Gerald shares as follows:
Remember the previous generations
*When we came to the country of our calling more than 30 years ago, we witnessed a generational change in our team. Wonderful servants that had been sacrificially labouring for 20, 30 and more years mainly in the medical field were about to return to their home country. They handed over the baton to us. As a historically and spiritually thinking person, I became aware of the privilege and responsibility to walk in the footsteps of **those that have gone before us.** We owe them much as they earned the trust of the local people through their commitment, sacrifice, faith and love. I have learned to honour those that have gone before us. There is immeasurable value in our diachronic heritage.*

Remember to invest in local Christians

Being aware of my own cultural and professional limitations, I have sought the constant fellowship and close cooperation with my local brothers and sisters. God has provided us with wonderful **local Christians** that have become stakeholders of the ministry. Their social, cultural, linguistic, mental and economic proximity proves crucial to an effective ministry. To invest in them in terms of discipleship, member care and professional training is inevitable to maintain or achieve greater excellence.

Remember the God-given vision
It is crucial to constantly remember, reflect and refocus on the **core vision** of our ministry. This may mean to return to the original vision or to modify and adapt the vision to a new situation under the guidance of the Holy Spirit.
We are supposed to ask the hard questions. Are we still effectively communicating the Gospel to our primary audience? Have theological, financial, administrative, structural or power issues darkened our vision? Do we clearly proclaim Jesus crucified and as the only way to eternal salvation or do we compromise for the sake of keeping relationships?

Remember to focus on being rather than doing
It is part of being young and energetic that "acting" gains priority over "being". However, as I have become older and stand back and reflect on our ministry life it becomes more important who I am in my **relationship with Jesus**. "Being" has gained priority over "doing". I long more and more to reflect Jesus to others. To make this paradigm shift I simply need to come back to the basics and to spend more time with HIM: reading his word, taking more time in prayer and spending time with people that have the same deep desire to grow in their intimate relationship with their Lord. To reflect Jesus well also means for me to live a morally pure life, to receive and extend forgiveness, to humbly look for reconciliation with others, to allow for the transformation of my character more and more into HIS image.

FORTITUDE – our courage

This exercise develops our capacity to endure in times of trial and when all odds seem to be against us. To develop courage in ministry and overcome the fear of man.

Deuteronomy 31:6 *"Be strong and courageous. Do not be afraid or terrified because of them, for the LORD our God goes with you; he will never leave you nor forsake you."*

JOSHUA AND LYDIE are a couple who have pioneered Discipleship Training Schools in Egypt, founded and directed Christian publishing ministries across the Arab World, translated, printed and distributed Christian literature in Arabic, launched numerous mercy ministries and are currently running a Conference and Training Centre in the North of Egypt. Through many years of ministry they were always subjected to threats and intimidation. Many times they had to "clean" their house of "sensitive documents" and had to destroy them discreetly. Even in the midst of several death threats they never gave up the joy of serving the Lord by serving His people.

Joshua and Lydie share as follows:
When we left Switzerland with our young baby daughter Rachelle in July 1987, little did we know what our future may hold. Our first step was Cyprus where we got involved in training young people, but Cyprus was not really the place of our calling. In 1989, we therefore moved to Egypt to lead the very 1st DTS (Discipleship Training School) in our country. As we were preparing, many people told us that Security will not be happy about this matter and will stop us. In spite of all these threats, we felt that God was leading us in this direction.
Through His Grace, we led the first DTS in a Coptic monastery in the South of Egypt, but the pressure from the security was big towards the leaders of the monastery. The consequences came rapidly and at the end of the course they informed us that we cannot run any further course with them. It was

not an easy situation but we decided to persevere and continue against all odds and at all costs.

We managed to lead a 2nd DTS with an Evangelical Church but again the pressure was big on the leadership of the church and therefore we were informed that they cannot receive us for any future courses. Again we had to find a different place to run our next DTS. Our situation was challenging and the only way to keep going was to look to the people, and entire matter through the eyes of God. He gave us new courage, a new vision and He extended our capacity in a miraculous way.

The 3rd DTS was organised with a Franciscan monastery. As we experienced it before, the security was heavy on all of us, on the students and staff. In spite of all our hardships, we had lots of space to receive guests, outreach teams, etc.

After these three experiences, we started to seek the Lord for a long- term solution for our future training courses and we felt that the Lord is leading us to the western desert. Everybody was against the idea of going to the desert and even after we bought the 1st piece of land, some of the leaders told us to give it to someone else. But again the Lord encouraged us to go ahead and not to stop.

Starting a place of prayer in this desert region was very difficult. We faced hard circumstances especially our needs of clean water. Then we went through the arduous negotiations with the Bedouins, the challenging dealings with security and the watchful eyes of the authorities. We suddenly faced more challenges and real opposition than before.
This was only the beginning of what we were going to go through. The questionings by officials and the bulldozers which came many times to destroy what we just had built was almost unbearable. In the midst of this, the Lord gave us a simple faith and willingness to follow Him regardless of the cost involved.

In 2012 when we received death threats, we entered into a new level of our capacity of courage. During this time, we went through true agony, fear, lots of uncertainties, danger and intimidations but God gave us courageous strength to continue our service. If we had listened to fear, we would have lost everything.

Today our centre became a large centre for conferences, seminars, training courses but also a place of refuge for many people who go through difficulties. Our facility is now officially recognised by the authorities and is guarded 24 hours a day by guards who are paid by the authorities!

The lessons we learned firstly is to be tuned in to the Lord's guidance and voice, then obey and act; the Lord honours faith. Secondly, we need to persevere and endure and this brings a new understanding and vision. We also learnt that we always need to look to the people and circumstances through the eyes of God.

We went through many difficult times but God was faithful and gave us supernatural grace and a divine capacity of courage to keep going.

When we are very young, exams are very simple, but once we are doing a Doctorate, the exam is very serious and hard. No one likes exams but we like the result when it's positive. Let's not give up, but endure.

LATITUDE – our flexibility

This exercise develops our capacity to be free, flexible and adaptable for the sake of the Gospel.

1 Corinthian 9:19-23 Though I am free and belong to no one, I have made myself a slave to everyone, to win as many as possible. To the Jews I became like a Jew, to win the Jews. To those under the law I became like one under the law... To those not having the law I became like one not having the law ... To the weak I became weak, to win the weak. I have become all things to all people so that by all possible means I might save some. I do all this for the sake of the gospel, that I may share in its blessings.

JOHNNY LI grew up in Hong Kong, abandoned and bitter. His mother was trapped inside China for 11 years, and he soon became involved with organized crime, running with a gang called the Triad Society. He stole, fought, and even practised magic and mystical arts.

At the age of 18 Johnny came to know Christ and even though he was free from his past, he had to adapt to his new purpose in life. After meeting a Christian who had escaped from China, Johnny suddenly felt drawn to visit China, and it made a lasting impression on him. People were hungry for Bibles and he realized he could not simply turn away and try to explain that he was just an ordinary Christian and that God had not called him to help.

Johnny began working as a volunteer to link foreigners and Chinese believers working with different churches and organizations. He joined a ministry and began to establish a network for distributing literature inside China. In 1991, Johnny was responsible for developing and compiling the first Bible Storybook in modern Mandarin for children. But the ministry was becoming almost too successful. With hundreds of thousands of Bibles being delivered, his activities came under surveillance by the central government. It became clear that he would be in danger if he travelled to China again. In 1996 his family relocated to the United States so that he could share with the free world what God was doing in the suffering church in China. Johnny and his family's flexibility was again stretched to the limit.

Today Johnny heads up a new ministry; Nexus Missions, with the primary vision being to help mainland Chinese churches send missionaries overseas—not to replace these churches' roles as senders, but to assist them with training, logistical support, and finances until they can become mature. Now, more than ten years later, Nexus has offices in the US and Hong Kong and has helped establish Nexus Mission Brazil. They are assisting missionaries working in nine countries of East, Southeast, and Central Asia; the Middle East; and Africa. Most of their work focuses on reaching out to refugees and slum dwellers.

Johnny shares as follows:
Trembling, I picked up the receiver of the ringing telephone. The familiar caller's voice was shaking with desperation: "You've got to help me get out of China NOW! I've been hiding for a year, fleeing from one province to the next, from one village to another. Just now I've escaped out the back because police were at the front door to arrest me. I can't keep taking this kind of pressure! My wife and I are both on the verge of a breakdown. Please help us!"

I had no words to comfort my co-worker. Hanging up, I could only weep.

Arriving in America, my family of four moved into an empty two-bedroom apartment. We only had our luggage with us containing the most precious of all our former belongings. I looked around at the bare walls, wondering when we'd be able to furnish the empty house. But in my heart, I felt even emptier.

The phone call I received just before leaving--those desperate, shaking voices...kept ringing in my ears and Satan kept on accusing me, "They stuck with you through fire and flood...how could you abandon them? How come you're the only one who runs away to freedom, when they've suffered much more than you? You're so selfish!"

Driven by accusation and self-blame I just couldn't bear the continual thoughts of my co-workers' suffering and the constant reminders of their suffering while I was living in freedom. I knew my newfound liberation could so easily turn into a limitation so I begged God to cast me to the very bottom...because then the only way to go would be up.

What helped me to extend my capacity in my new surroundings was the realisation that it hadn't been my will to flee: God had called me. So when I was unable to bear those thoughts any longer, He showed me His purpose, that I would be a voice for my brothers who had gone through the fire, who had no voice of their own. My freedom would become their freedom, as I considered their prison my prison. Though now in different worlds, we couldn't be separated in spirit by any national border!

After that, though sometimes my thoughts still accused me, I no longer got discouraged. The Lord continued to encourage me. Now, I could never leave Him or His calling! He is the greatest, and His will is the highest. I will serve Him all my life!

- Johnny is the President and CEO of **Nexus Mission**, a ministry with the primary vision of helping mainland Chinese churches to send missionaries overseas—not to replace these churches' roles as senders, but to assist them with training, logistical support, and finances until they can become mature. Contact Johnny for teaching and speaking: johnny1956@gmail.com or http://nexusmission.website/en/

QUIETUDE – our calmness

This exercise develops our capacity to be still, not quiet and passive, but a confident stillness based on faith and contentment.

Psalm 46:10 He says, "Be still, and know that I am God; I will be exalted among the nations, I will be exalted in the earth."

HANNELIE GROENEWALD is a former Christian Aid Worker in Kabul who lost her entire family in a horrific terror attack when three Taliban members entered their house and killed her husband, Werner, and two children, JP and Rodé. The men then set the house on fire. Hannelie is the author of the book "Terreur in Kaboel" (Terror in Kabul).

Hannelie shares as follows:
It was actually during and after the attack while being back in SA that I've realized my capacity to rest in the Lord has grown tremendously. As if the tragic experience in Kabul prepared me for it.

So many challenges and heartache came in my life during and after the event, and although heartbroken, I've strangely accepted whatever the Lord would allow in my life and for whatever reason He deemed necessary. I didn't have the desire to be in control like before. Control is something I've surrendered to the Lord years ago. In a huge way it freed me of any guilt I possibly could have had about being obedient to God's call to go to Afghanistan and subsequently what happened on 29 Nov 2014, because I would never consider moving forward if I haven't prayed about it and waited upon the Lord for answers and confirmation.

Calmness comes from total surrender and faith *in our loving God. It sets you free and produces that calmness that is only found in the Lord.*

FAITH calms you in the midst of a storm; it doesn't take you out of the storm, but helps you through it. It gives you the power to hold on in the toughest of times. It produces resilience, persistence and calmness; the ability to keep going. You won't be able to survive without resilience. Where do you get it from? By having faith in our Almighty God who is able to accomplish anything through us and use our circumstances whether good or bad. It is that simple.

Trusting God wholeheartedly and submitting to His perfect will for your life will ultimately demand that you step out of your comfort zone of trying to control your own life, while stretching your faith to a new level. This will produce the calmness everybody is looking for in the eye of the storm.

Hannelie is the author of the book TERREUR IN KABOEL. It tells of a woman living in obedience, only to find the foundations of her faith rocked. The book will inspire the reader to count the true cost of our faith, and to reflect on the character of God and our identity as His children. Hannelie's story is a remarkable testimony of a life in faith and the power of forgiveness. Website: http://www.nb.co.za/Books/20118

RECTITUDE – our righteousness

This exercise develops our capacity in **righteousness.** Our understanding of righteousness must expand our capacity to reach beyond our emotional, national and cultural borders.

Psalm 48:10 Like your name, O God, your praise reaches to the ends of the earth; your right hand is filled with righteousness.

PASTOR CHRISTO WALTERS is considered one of the leading missions mobilizers in South Africa. He travels frequently to countries with the most unreached and unengaged people groups to mobilize the local believers to reach out to their own unreached.

Christo shares as follows:
To be called by God to full time ministry from a successful business background and then struggling to be fruitful in the ministry, posed a huge challenge to me.

I loved the Lord so much, but all my endeavours brought so little fulfilment. John 15 verse 7 haunted me: "By this my Father is glorified, that you bear much fruit"

*I soon realized my outer man was a huge hindrance and made me unable to submit to the Spirit's control thus rendering me incapable to obey God's commands. **I realized my outer man needed to be broken.***

Out of desperation I sought God and He led me to a time of fasting and praying. This discipline exercised through the years enabled God to deal with the breaking of my outer man. Thus making a way for God's Spirit to be released through my quickened and controlled spirit.

During these times of fasting and praying God shared His heart with me for the lost, unreached and the suffering. I was continually envisioned by God revealing His heart and purposes to me.   My capacity expanded and God led me to mobilize literally hundreds of churches to the task of missions.

*To be obedient to the Spirit became the norm and not the exception anymore. Any measure of fruitfulness requires the breaking of the outer man to allow the release of the spirit. The breaking of the soul's power is imperative if the human spirit is to express the life of the Lord Jesus.   **The Lord uses for His glory those servants who are most perfectly broken**.*

The Lord teaches us the following in Scripture:
I choose to be around those whose carnal strength is broken who need Me and cling to Me. All the rebellion in them is crushed and they are gentle, submissive, believing and resting on every word I say. Fellowship with them is easy – is no power struggle.
Isaiah 57 verse 15.

The soft and tender hearted is the person I am looking for. He knows his need of me. He has the utmost respect for My word, giving, honoring, believing and adhering to it. He lives by every word that proceeds out of my mouth.
Isaiah 66 verse 2

SERVITUDE – our servanthood

This exercise develops our capacity not only to serve the Lord, but to become servants of all.

Mark 9:35 Sitting down, Jesus called the Twelve and said, "Anyone who wants to be first must be the very last, and the servant of all."

HB BAJGAI, affectionally known simply as HB to all his friends, came to know Christ from a Hindu background in Bhutan after being miraculously delivered from demonic dreams. HB immediately started sharing his new-found faith with his fellow Bhutanese, one of the most unreached people-groups in the world. Bhutan is a mountainous region where most people live an hour's walk from the nearest road and travelling to villages to share the Gospel always involves hours of trekking through forests in extreme circumstances. HB heads up the network of Churches in Bhutan and is involved in various projects in uplifting communities, Church planting, discipleship projects and mercy ministries

HB shares as follows:
All Glory to our Lord and Saviour, Jesus Christ, who left His comfort zone to become a servant. One cannot explain or fully understand how God could come down from His precious, awesome, beautiful Heaven to the sinful and corrupt world. But He left such a comfort zone and came down to such a sinful, restless place and transformed Himself into a human being to save and serve mankind. Now that the Living God is dwelling with men, they will be His people and God Himself will be with them and be their God. Once the Spirit of such a living God is in us, we feel His command, the command of most high God, to be His messengers and His servants.

How do we know and feel that we are called by God? We recognise our calling when we start feeling pity for the unsaved, innocent people around us, in every place, in every remote village, wherever the harvest is ready.

Joshua 1:9 "Have I not commanded you? Be strong and courageous. Do not be frightened, and do not be dismayed, for the Lord your God is with you wherever you go."

As soon as we started feeling the leading of the Holy Spirit with such a clear indication to be the messenger for Christ, it moved us away from our comfort zones to witness Christ with a deep inner burning desire and with tears in our eyes. It also reminded us of our own first day of conversion and how God sent someone to bring Good News to us and how He revealed Himself in our dreams and delivered us completely from the demonic attacks. It was Jesus Himself who appeared in my dream on the night of my conversion. It was a very bright light with a person standing in the middle of the light with a long white garment. No matter how much I tried to look at the face, I couldn't identify Him because it was a glorious face, shining like a bright morning Star. He walked towards me and touched me and the demon which was terrorizing me for such a long time left my body and I was completely delivered from such demonization. While I was seeing this dream, I felt that I was raised from the dead and transformed to heaven. It was so peaceful, comforting, so heavenly and calm and there was nothing I needed. I thought to myself that if heaven is indeed the best place to go to then why did it take me so long to discover this? My heart was filled with gratitude.

But if we want to see miracles, if we desire to see the Word in action, then we have to move outside our comfort zones. There are thousands and thousands of people who need you and God wants you to be the vessel and the hero in the midst of them, like Moses the deliverer. The amazing thing is that God Himself will go before you and hold your hand for miracles after miracles, healings after healings, conversions after conversions. Loving kindness and feelings of giving to the needy will follow. You will only feel that your blessings are overflowing and that you want to extend these blessings to others and give more, even give everything that you have. The God of Heaven will double your portion of blessings and will refill your store house as you build more store houses to bless others.

Isaiah 42:16 'And I will lead the blind in a way that they do not know, in paths that they have not known I will guide them. I will turn the darkness before them into light, the rough places into level ground. These are the things I do, and I do not forsake them.'

On 29 September 1995, on the day of my water baptism, a bright light showed me many villages and I saw a huge crowd of people who were in darkness. Now every new village or remote place in Bhutan I go to I feel that those are the places I have already seen in my dream in the year 1995. Some time we feel so tired and ask the God of Heaven why we have to be so busy and sometimes feel so empty. God answered our prayers through the encouragement of so many friends living overseas or outside of Bhutan. As soon as we receive such emails & messages then we are filled with new strength, motivated and we feel like going back to the unreached areas to continue the work and serve.

HB is also the CEO of Peaceful Tours in Bhutan. You can contact HB to support his ministry, explore Bhutan or invite him to speak at your church:
Website: www.bhutanpeacefultour.com,
Email: hastainhim@gmail.com

SOLICITUDE – our attentiveness

This exercise develops our capacity to listen and to be attentive to God's purposes when we meet people and watch the news.

Proverbs 1:5 let the wise listen and add to their learning, and let the discerning get guidance.

DR DAVID AIKMAN has had a long and successful career as a journalist. Perhaps the most well-known aspect of that career was his 23 years at TIME Magazine, with reporting spanning the globe of nearly all the major historical events of the time. Dr Aikman began his reporting career with TIME Magazine in 1971. In the 23 years that followed, he reported from five continents and more than 55 countries, and wrote three consecutive Man of the Year cover stories. As a TIME Magazine senior correspondent and foreign correspondent, he interviewed numerous major world figures, from Mother Teresa to Manuel Noriega, from Alexander Solzhenitsyn to Pham Van Dong, from Boris Yeltsin to Billy Graham. Dr Aikman was assigned to bureaus in Hong Kong, from where he covered the entire Asian region; in Beijing, China; in Berlin, Germany, where he covered all of Eastern Europe; and in Jerusalem, Israel, where he covered the entire Middle East. He was bureau chief in Berlin, Jerusalem and Beijing before returning to the United States to cover the State Department until his departure in 1994 to devote his time to writing books.

David shares as follows:
*The most meaningful learning experience from my life of extensive travel and multiple encounters with Christian believers in many different parts of the world is this: **listen with a large sense of humility and a servant spirit but listen attentively to what they tell you.***

It is easy for a visitor to various countries where there is persecution and perhaps oppression to think that one is bringing to these believers largess from afar. But it was only when I stopped to listen carefully to what they were saying that I understood they were often giving me much more than I was giving them. I remember after visiting believers in Eastern Europe and Russia a few times several years ago, I was struck by how much I was able to learn about their societies simply by listening to them carefully. By asking questions about the different struggles they had in daily life, I learned what the most difficult points of their lives were. That gave me an insight into how their entire society was functioning.

On the other hand, Christian maturity goes both ways. Many Christians visiting China from outside in recent years have been so struck by the daily challenges the Chinese face that they forget that they had something to give to the Chinese. A few years ago I was in a group of mature American believers who had an opportunity to share our considerable experience of Christian living with much younger Chinese followers of Jesus. There is no question that the Chinese fellowship was blessed by our presence. It was good to see that Christian maturity is not merely a function of the degree of suffering that one experiences for living out the faith. We were blessed on both sides, but those of us from the West who emerged from these meetings realized more vividly than before what a rich tapestry the Body of Christ is throughout the world and how it is possible to give out in a variety of ways what one has previously received.

David is also the author of a number of highly acclaimed books, the latest being WHEN THE ALMOND TREE BLOSSOMS, a timely novel after the 2016 USA presidential election that politically polarized the nation more than since the Civil War. This book is a reminder of what's at stake: not only freedom, but life and peace.
Website: http://davidaikman.com/
Email: dbtaikman@gmail.com

In closing, my humble advice is simple.
When it comes to your life, and your pursuit for the
cause of Christ, give everything, or give nothing.
He wants it all.
Seek above all things the joy of intimacy and pursue
above all things the capacity to contain more and the
ability to reflect more.
Don't waste your life on the insignificant.

One of my all-time favourite prayers for capacity growth is the one prayed by Sir Francis Drake, an adventurer, as he departed to the west coast of South America.

Disturb us, Lord,
When we are too pleased with ourselves,
When our dreams have come true because we dreamed too little,
When we arrived safely because we sailed too close to the shore.
Disturb us, Lord,
When with the abundance of things we possess we have lost our thirst for the waters of life;
When, having fallen in love with life, we have ceased to dream of eternity And in our efforts to build a new earth, we have allowed our vision of the new Heaven to dim.
Disturb us, Lord,
To dare more boldly,
to venture on wilder seas where storms will show Your mastery;
Where losing sight of land, we shall find the stars.

We ask you to push back the horizons of our hopes;
And to push back the future in strength, courage, hope, and love.
This we ask in the name of our Captain, who is Jesus Christ.

IN*context* International

"From Issachar came men who understood the times and knew what Israel should do." (1 Chronicles 12:32)

"Understanding the times" was one of the key components in establishing the kingdom of David. Interpreting the seasons and knowing what to do still remains one of the key components in establishing the Kingdom of God on earth.

The fall of communism, the rise of extremism, the growth of atheism and the new face of Islam are shaping the world we live in. A split in global powers over chemical weapons and a global threat of nuclear weapons will impact the globe in a definitive way. New leaders in Europe and the US, millions of refugees on the move from East to West, the 'Back to Jerusalem Movement' from China and the decline of Christianity in Europe will have a profound effect on missions. In the midst of a new spiritual climate, the Arab Spring and multiple wars in the Middle East, Islam finds itself at a crossroads and is presenting the Church with unprecedented opportunities.

In a time such as this, the Church cannot afford to be ill-informed. God is on the move, and every and any mission activity should reflect this. Without identifying trends, our activities will not bear fruit that lasts.

To take missions to the absolute extreme will require men and women of valour who are equipped with knowledge and clothed with wisdom. The Lord never failed to warn His disciples, time and time again, to watch and to be alert (e.g. Mark 13, Luke 12).

Consider the following points in relation to your current mission programmes:

- God cannot lead you on the basis of information that you do not have. Information is critical for project planning and decision making.

- Information for its own sake is worthless; valuable information is that which can be converted into meaningful action.
- Not all information is created equal: some information is accurate and adds value; some unreliable and potentially harmful.
- We cannot make good decisions if we have bad information. This is critical for lasting involvement.
- More information is not the same as useful information.
- The earlier in the decision-making process we have good information, the wider our range of options for productive programmes.
- Good information improperly or inaccurately interpreted leaves us worse off than if we had no information.
- Information without context is usually misleading.
- Great strategy is built on current and accurate information, placed in a proper context, interpreted within that context, and resulting in specific and targeted behaviour.

This is where IN*context* comes in...

Our vision is to assist and empower churches and mission-minded believers to interpret world events and global trends within a Kingdom context. Gathering meaningful information and interpreting emerging trends becomes the foundation for lasting and meaningful involvement. Anyone can obtain information, but it takes time, effort and skill to gather the right information and to explain it in a proper, understandable and meaningful fashion.

IN*context* International has dedicated staff who serve the mission community by doing this. We are committed to providing news in a non-sensational, accurate, truthful and verified manner.

Our mission is to INVESTIGATE global news, INTERPRET events from a Biblical perspective, INFORM mission-minded believers and assist churches to contemplate strategic and lasting INVOLVEMENT.

INVESTIGATE
IN*context* International's dedicated and skilled staff endeavour to investigate global news and world trends to find what is helpful, accurate, verified and useful.

INTERPRET
IN*context* International further endeavours, with the assistance of local believers and trusted sources, to interpret events from a Biblical perspective and connect the dots into a cohesive picture so that churches can respond strategically, timeously and purposefully.

INFORM
IN*context* International makes this information and related resources available to the Christian community free of charge. The team is available to present seminars, conferences and workshops within the Christian community to inform, inspire and assist believers with an understanding of the world in a Kingdom context.

INVOLVE
IN*context* International ultimately aims to facilitate strategic involvement in regions of influence, to aid believers who are instruments of hope and agents of peace.

What IN*context* offers:
With more than 30 years' experience in missions, IN*context* International offers resources that enable churches, missions committees and individuals to interpret world events and global trends within a Kingdom context.

With countless visits to the Arab world, Asia, South East Asia, Africa and the Gulf, the content of our resources are shaped by the perspectives gained from interviewing local leaders and missionaries.

Resources include:

- *A World in Context* – seminars, tailored for your group, with contextual information from strategic regions. Contact Mike Burnard for more information: 0828657380
- *A World in Motion* – a bi-weekly news update on current events from a missions perspective (free subscription)
- *Website* – daily up-to-date information on global news, perspectives and information
- *Pray for the Nations* – a weekly prayer PowerPoint focusing on current events and contemporary issues
- *Strategic projects* – based on research and initiated by Christian leaders in restricted areas

If you would like more information on any aspect of this book, or about any other of the resources available, please do not hesitate to contact Mike Burnard or the team.

Other books available:

- *The 18 Inch Principle*
- *Dancing with Camels*
- *Catcrackers*
- *Reflections*

COPYRIGHT

You are most welcome to contact the author if you would like to use portions of this book for public use. To use quotes in the book from other authors, it would be best to contact the original sources directly for permission.

There is a special request ...

This book would not have been possible without the lives and testimonies of countless Christians who have paid the ultimate price for our faith. They desperately depend on us for support and prayers. If you make use of the information in this book, please consider sponsoring some of our projects in restricted countries.

Please contact us if you want to make a contribution. We will then supply you with the necessary banking details.

INcontext
INTERNATIONAL

P.O. Box 3197, Durbanville, 7551
South Africa

You are welcome to contact the author:
mike@incontextministries.org

Website:
www.incontextinternational.org

www.ingramcontent.com/pod-product-compliance
Lightning Source LLC
Chambersburg PA
CBHW051818090426
42736CB00011B/1545